The
Seven
Human
Powers

The Seven Human Powers

Luminous Shadows of the Self

Shirley J. Nicholson

Quest Books
Theosophical Publishing House

Wheaton, Illinois ♦ Chennai (Madras), India

The Theosophical Society in America acknowledges with gratitude the generous support of the Kern Foundation for the publication of this book.

The Theosophical Publishing House
P. O. Box 270
Wheaton, Illinois 60189-0270

Cover and book design by Kirsten Hansen

Library of Congress Cataloging-in-Publication Data

Nicholson, Shirley J.
Seven human powers: luminous shadows of the self / Shirley J. Nicholson.--1st Quest ed.
  p.   cm.
Includes bibliographical references and index.
ISBN 0-8356-0829-8
1. Self—Religious aspects—Theosophy.   2. Theosophy—Doctrines.
I. Title.

BP573.M3 N53 2003
299'.934--dc21   2002036943

Printed in the United States of America

5   4   3   2   1   *   03   04   05   06   07   08

Table of Contents

I, verily, am Brahman, the One without a second, which, like the sky, is beginningless and endless, in which the whole universe . . . appears to be a mere shadow.

Shankaracharya, The Crest Jewel of Wisdom

Not only did the Sun itself produce cave and fire and moving shapes, and the shadows, and their beholders, but in doing so it manifested a property of its own nature not less essential—even more excellent—than that pure radiance upon which no earthly eye could steadfastly gaze. The shadows were as needful to the Sun as the Sun to the shadows; their existence was the very consummation of its perfection.

Plato, The Republic

Preface

The baseball player Yogi Berra is reported to have said, "You've got to be careful if you don't know where you're going because you won't get there." That quirkily stated truth might be paraphrased as "You've got to be careful if you don't know who you are because you won't be yourself."

I have wanted to write a know-who-you-are book ever since *Ancient Wisdom—Modern Insight* was published in 1985. In that book, I drew on both Theosophy and contemporary knowledge for an overview of what the cosmos is and where it is going as it takes us along for the ride. Since then, I have wanted to expand on its chapter about who it is that's taking the ride and why we are doing so anyway.

It has taken me many years to find the time to turn that wish into reality. But those years have seen an explosion of consciousness studies in a number of fields. Psychology has plumbed new depths of the psyche and spirit. Psychotherapy has worked with even the highest reaches of human consciousness. Meditation has become readily available at many depths. We have never had a richer climate in which to explore human nature.

I have plucked some fruits from this plentiful tree and tried to share them in simple and lucid language. "To write well," Aristotle said, "express yourself like the common people but think like a wise person." The reader must be the judge of what wisdom is in this book, but I believe that I think like a Theosophist and hope I have conveyed some part of Theosophical wisdom. Theosophy offers an accurate and detailed map of all that we are, but we ourselves must explore the territory that the map represents.

In recent years, my own exploration has been in the study of Buddhism and the practice of Buddhist meditation. That influence pervades this book, which is less metaphysical and more experiential than *Ancient Wisdom—Modern Insight*. I believe, as did the Buddha, that to be ourselves and to find our way, we need to know who we are. Seeking self-knowledge is not a waste of time or selfishness but down-to-earth and practical. It has results in the world. As Swami Nikhilananda says in the preface to his translation of Shankaracharya's *Self-Knowledge:* "Self-knowledge is vital. All other forms of knowledge are of secondary importance; for a man's action, feeling, reasoning, and thinking are dependent on his idea of the Self" (xv). He goes on to say that if people believe themselves to be material creatures, they will follow a selfish ideal of material happiness and pleasure. If they believe they are spiritual entities with material bodies that should be used for spiritual ends, they will follow a path of love and unselfishness and promote peace and happiness for all.

If we explore our stream of consciousness, we find both material and spiritual levels, from the densest physical to the empty fullness of the highest spiritual, from the fragmentary and separative levels to absolute unity. We find familiar powers such as thought, emotion, and intuition all interblended into a structured whole, with every part interacting with all the others. We find a whole universe within ourselves, for as the Chandogya Upanishad says, "Even so large as the universe outside is the universe within the lotus of the heart. Within it are heaven and earth, the sun and the moon, the lightning and all the stars. What is in the macrocosm is in the microcosm also" (Prabhavananda 74). And at the heart of this inner universe, as with the outer one, we find we are one with a divine field of consciousness, with Brahman or God.

So returning to Yogi Berra's wisdom, finding out who we are is finding out where we are going. We are on our way home, to our inmost roots, to realization of our oneness with all. And we *will* get there, for our final destination is what we already are but only need to discover.

Psyche and Cosmos

The heart is the dwelling place of that which is the essence of the universe. . . . If you draw aside the veils of the stars and the spheres, you will see that all is one with the Essence of your own pure soul.

Farid al-Din Attar

Many stories are told about Nasrudin, the wise fool of Sufi tales. Some of them are traditional and ancient, and some have a contemporary flavor, undoubtedly invented more recently. In one story of the latter sort, Nasrudin goes to the bank to cash a check. The teller asks him for identification. So Nasrudin whips out a mirror from his pocket, looks into it, and says, "Oh, yeah, that's me, all right."

We are often like Nasrudin. In our times, we are under the admonition inscribed at the entrance to the shrine of the Delphic oracle: "Know thyself." But if someone asks us who we are, we are likely to say something like, "I'm a teacher," or "a business person," or "an American," or "a liberal." We tend to look superficially at a reflection of ourselves in our accomplishments and role in the world, at what we do rather than what we are in our innermost being. Like Nasrudin, we say, "Oh, yeah, that's me."

Our century has seen unprecedented development in knowledge about the psyche, our inner being. We know that there are aspects of our inner life of which we are not conscious. We know the almost insuperable strength of automatic habits formed by conditioning. We are becoming aware of the powerful connection of our bodies with our thoughts, attitudes, and emotions, especially with regard to health. We are learning about extrasensory perception, by which people know things they have had no opportunity to learn through the usual channels. We have even glimpsed states of consciousness in which superhuman feats are possible and states of meditation in which profound alterations of mental and bodily functions have been measured. Psychology has unearthed a wealth of information that helps us know and understand ourselves.

The Hidden Structure of Human Nature

Yet there are still depths and layers within us that psychology is only beginning to suspect. Sigmund Freud introduced the concept of the subconscious as the realm of our worst antisocial selves, the sewer of the mind and heart. C. G. Jung expanded that idea to include the collective unconscious, including the memories and capacities that all humans have shared since the birth of humankind. Roberto Assagioli and other more recent transpersonal psychologists have added the concept of the superconscious, the part of ourselves that, though unconscious, is grander and more noble than our ordinary conscious selves. Transpersonal psychology now includes parts of the Self that transcend the individual—universal experiences of higher consciousness that are not limited to a personal mind.

Traditional wisdom has inspired some recent psychologists, whose work is throwing new light on human nature and enriching the knowledge that has come down to us through the ages. An adept teacher of modern Theosophy offered "to exhume the primeval strata of man's being, his basic nature, and lay bare the wonderful complications of his inner self—something never to be achieved by . . . psychology in its ultimate expression" (*Mahatma Letters* 68). Yet transpersonal psychologists are exploring just such "primeval strata."

Some parts of the "primeval strata" have already been discovered. C. G. Jung defined four human functions: sensation, feeling, intuition, and thinking. Huston Smith (60–95), an authority on the world's religions, writes of four levels in nature and in humans that most spiritual traditions recognize. The highest is the infinite, the celestial void, unbounded, undifferentiated. The next level is the celestial, in which individual minds can be distinguished from the universal mind, although they are not separate from it. The third level is the intermediate or psychic plane, the locus of subtle bodies. And the lowest is the terrestrial plane, whose dense material bodies derive from the subtler ones of the third level. Esoteric traditions throughout history have understood in precise detail the many functions and levels of consciousness. They offer a model for the realms that comprise the human psyche, with its depths and shallows, its beauties and horrors. These traditions have also taught us how to develop latent aspects of the self and how to awaken our finer unconscious potentials.

Buddhism, for example, refers to material and psychic elements or "aggregates" that make up the individual mind-body. They are the physical body, feelings, perceptions, mental formations (or emotions and thoughts), and consciousness of the other aggregates. Vedanta philosophy teaches about "sheaths," which are bodies or vehicles of consciousness at various levels. They include a "food sheath," the physical body; a sheath made of vital forces (*prana*); a sheath for the mind and senses, including emotions; a sheath of higher understanding; and a sheath of bliss. The ancient Egyptians knew how various aspects of personality function in life and death. They held that the physical body is inhabited by the *ba,* its animating principle of spirit, and the *ka,* the magnetic powers we call the personality, which can gravitate to either the higher or lower principles; as well as a number of other powers, including the shade or ghost (*khaibit),* which persists for a while after death. Plato taught that the passions and affections are at different levels within us and have different functions in our lives. Today we might say that the passions are personal and what he called the affections are transpersonal, or not limited only to our personal concerns.

Human Powers

Theosophy, which is a modern statement of the wisdom of esoteric philosophy, offers a clear and comprehensive map of the different layers and functions of the human psyche. These basic powers are termed "principles." Principles are not things but rather powers or ways in which our consciousness can function. All the principles are inherent in everyone. Some principles are developed and consciously used. Others are partially developed and used only to a limited extent. Some are only potential and not used at all. Some principles have not yet dawned into human consciousness, except in a few rare individuals who are ahead of our species as a whole.

The principles include the physical body; the emotional or desire nature (*kama* in Sanskrit, also called the "astral body"); the mind (*manas)* with its concrete, everyday functions and its abstract, philosophical aspects; intuition and a sense of unity (*buddhi*); and pure consciousness (*atma*), which is the ground of being and encompasses will in its most profound sense: the will to be.

All the other principles are inherent in the last, atma, which is their spiritual core. If we think of ourselves as atma, as pure consciousness without content, just knowingness or the ability to be aware, we might think of the principles as television channels on different frequencies that we can access. When we as atma tune in to WBOD, for instance, we feel the gurgling in our stomach, our chest rising and falling as we breathe, our muscles contracting as we walk. All our senses come into sharp focus. We see how the green of the pine is different from the green of the oak. We are aware of the fragrance of a rose and the pungency of onions. The tinkle of the wind chimes and the auditory quality of our partner's voice come in loud and clear. We are acutely aware of physicality and sense experience.

When we tune in to KICK, we get emotional highs and lows as our emotions rise and fall. Peppy music exhilarates us, or news of a friend's misfortune overwhelms us with sorrow. We are aware of those nuances of anxiety, jealousy, or irritation that we usually ignore. We are *in* our emotions.

KNOW highlights our intellect and thoughts. On this channel, a flash of memory reminds us to pick up our dry cleaning. Questions about changing our job stay on the screen for a while. A puzzlement appears, raised by a book we are studying. Here we are aware of thoughts of all kinds—logical and irrational, cosmic and personal, significant and trivial.

WAHA shows flashes of intuition. The screen may light up with a sudden insight as to the meaning of a recent illness and how we should change our lifestyle. We may see the cyclic nature of our life and of nature from a new perspective. Sometimes we may even see the oneness and unity among ourselves, nature, and the entire cosmos—or even within the PTA board, in spite of its heated disagreements.

Theosophical writings usually refer to seven principles. H. P. Blavatsky, a founder of the Theosophical Society and its seminal teacher, in her magnum opus, *The Secret Doctrine*, and in other writings, refers to seven principles. Two of the principles she lists are associated with the physical body: the "vital body" or "etheric double," the physical body's subtler counterpart, and the universal energy or life force *(prana)* that permeates every level of being, but is especially connected with the vital body. *Seven Human Powers* highlights five of the principles and covers the vital body and energy with the physical body in chapter 3. The Sanskrit terms for the principles are given below so that the reader may be familiar with them, as they are used in most Theosophical books. They are widely used because it is hard to find an exact English equivalent for many of them.

HUMAN POWERS

English term	Sanskrit term
Consciousness or spiritual will	Atma
Sense of unity or intuition	Buddhi
Mind, including	Manas
• Philosophical mind	• Higher manas
• Concrete mind	• Lower manas
Emotions	Kama
Physical body, including	Sthula sharira
• Life force	• Prana
• Vital body or field	• Linga sharira

TABLE I

These principles are amazing powers, but we take most of them for granted because they are so common. Even ordinary mental powers—such as memory, delivery of the word we want, or the ability to grasp an idea—are mysterious and almost miraculous. Neuropsychologists cannot explain them. But in a sense these powers are only shadows of our true identity. They reveal the light of atma, which, as Indian sage Shankaracharya says in *The Crest Jewel of Wisdom*, "causes all things to shine, but which all things cannot make to shine." Atma is the One Light that illumines all creation. The other principles reveal some of the powers of atma but are like two-dimensional representations or shadows that lack the fullness of the real thing. Still, the principles light up our inner being in the world. We can think of them as luminous shadows of our true being, or atma.

Consciousness and the One Life

According to Theosophy, as well as to Vedanta and other Indian systems, "The reality behind all is Brahman, pure consciousness," as the Indian sage Shankaracharya put it. Atma, which is also pure consciousness, is one with Brahman, the ultimate Reality. Individual consciousness in its pure, unclouded state is one with God or the One Life that sustains the cosmos. In Indian philosophy, this fundamental Reality is referred to as *sat-chit-ananda*: being, knowing or consciousness, and joy. Ultimate Reality is an unbroken continuum of consciousness, and consciousness, not matter, is primary, the ground of all being.

Leading scientists are finding support for this ancient idea in contemporary quantum physics. Saul-Paul Sirag says, "There is only one consciousness in a cosmic sense." Fred Alan Wolf concurs that there is "one basic consciousness in which we are all one" (Mishlove). Amit Goswami goes farther when he states that consciousness is primary. "Consciousness is the ground of being; it is the one and only, the absolute" (Goswami 72). This is the Theosophical position, and although these theorists do not claim to prove that position, their research and thought lends additional credence to the reality of one source-consciousness, from which comes everything that exists.

Although it is universal, this continuum also exists in individuals. As the Upanishads have it, atma is "greater than the great and smaller than the small." The states of consciousness we humans ordinarily experience are rooted in pure universal consciousness, but our minds become limited and clouded through involvement in our different principles and through conditioning. As Blavatsky (*Secret Doctrine* 1:15) put it, the One Reality is "the field of Absolute Consciousness, i.e., that Essence . . . of which conscious existence is a conditioned *symbol.*" It is, however, possible to break through the limits of individual consciousness to the boundless One, as seers and mystics have reported, for "the mind, sense organs, and so on, are illumined by atma alone," according to Shankaracharya (Nikhilandanda 143).

Intuition, mind, emotion, and body (with energy and form)—all the other principles—express something of the immense potential of atma. "The six principles [are] the outcome—the variously differentiated aspects—of the SEVENTH and ONE, the only reality in the Universe" (Blavatsky, *Secret Doctrine* 1:17). Although atma can be thought of as a continuum of consciousness, an unbroken field, it also expresses itself as points. Each individual is a point of localization in the universal field of atma. We can think of ourselves as a point in the eternal encased in different layers, the six lower principles, a white light surrounded by globes of different colors through which it shines.

Three Levels of Being

The six principles plus atma can be grouped into three aspects of ourselves: the personality, the transpersonal Self or soul, and the spiritual core or atma. Theosophy gives a precise meaning to the term "personality"; it combines the functions of the body, the vital body and its energy, the emotions and desires, and the concrete, everyday part of the mind. You can easily recognize this aspect of the self as you function in daily life. When you make a to-do list, when you feel a surge of anxiety or excitement, when you want an ice-cream cone or a new car, when you feel energized or depleted, you are experiencing aspects of the personality. It is the most familiar part of ourselves.

According to C. G. Jung, the soul or subjective "inner personality," which stands outside time and space, consists of a certain "limited complex of functions." In Theosophy, too, though the soul or transpersonal Self is seen somewhat differently than from Jung's view, it is not vague and unformed. It has specific powers: the abstract, philosophical mind; the intuition or unity sense; and the spiritual will. You are familiar with these functions in yourself, but you use them less often than those of the personality. When you get a sudden rush of compassion, when you reach to understand the nature of an abstract idea, when the solution to a persistent problem dawns on you, when you act heroically without thinking of yourself, when you resolve to follow a spiritual path, when you are taken out of yourself by music or a sunset, you are calling on the powers of the transpersonal Self. Ken Wilber, a principal theorist in the transpersonal movement, refers to this level of experience as a deeper within and a wider beyond.

The transpersonal Self serves as a bridge between the personality and the pure transcendent unity of atma where there is no separate self. It is the locus of individuality, the refraction of the One Light into an individual ray. Many Theosophical sources use the term *individuality* for that soul or transpersonal Self.

The myth of Narcissus illustrates the relation between the personality and the soul or transpersonal Self. In this story, Narcissus, who is a beautiful youth, sees his reflection in a fountain where he goes to drink. Believing the reflection to be the nymph of the fountain, he falls in love with it. When he smiles, the reflection smiles back at him, and when he opens his arms to it, the reflection opens its arms to him. But when he plunges his arms into the water to embrace it, the reflection flees from his touch. When he finds his beloved unattainable, he pines away, dies, and his shade turns into a flower.

The myth is usually interpreted as a warning against self-love and narcissism. But in Hermetic Gnostic versions of the story, the soul projects its image into the world. It then falls in love with the image and thus becomes captured by the world. The transpersonal Self mistakes its temporary reflection, the personality, as something real that can be grasped and held on to. We become attached to our reflection in the personality, forgetting who we truly are. The Tibetan teacher Nyoshul Khenpo understood the myth of Narcissus in a similar way; he says that "beings become alienated, confused (like Narcissus), and through their own ignorance get lost in self-deception" (110–11). The personality is only a temporary reflection of the soul. When we identify ourselves with it, we become limited to a small range of functions and powers and closed to our higher principles.

Atma, our deepest spiritual core, is outside the sphere of individual selfhood. It is universal and impersonal, one with the divine or Brahman, the one essence of all. We may have occasional intimations of the oneness of pure atma, which is consciousness itself, not colored by the principles, though normally we function only through the other principles.

Figure 2 depicts the principles grouped according to the levels of consciousness. Atma is represented in the chart as spiritual will, the will to be. The Theosophical teacher and social activist Annie Besant called will "the power aspect of consciousness." It is the charioteer that drives the horses of both the personality and the transpersonal Self.

THE PRINCIPLES, PERSONALITY, TRANSPERSONAL SELF

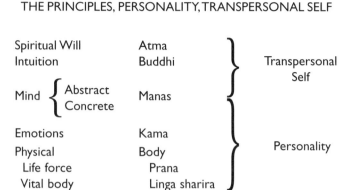

TABLE 2

Atma can also be thought of as the background on which table 2 is drawn, the consciousness behind each principle. Spiritual will brings into being the transpersonal Self, comprising intuition and the higher mind. From this level emanate the powers of the personality: lower mind, emotions, vital body, and energy. Finally, the physical body becomes solidified within these interpenetrating fields. Rather than reducing inner functions to the physical level as scientific materialism does, Theosophy and esoteric philosophy view the body as the outcome of the higher principles.

The transpersonal Self is a relatively permanent expression for the atmic consciousness as it is focused in each individual. From this level the personality is projected, and at death the locus of consciousness that we experience recedes to the level of the soul. After a period of gestation, another personality is projected into the world.

Interbeing

A human being, an animal, a plant, or even a stone cannot exist in isolation. The life of a maple tree in the forest, for example, depends on many other things. One of those is light from the sun, which travels through immense distances before it reaches the tree. The life cycle of the tree is coordinated with the earth's spin on its axis, which causes night and day, as the leaves give off oxygen in the light and carbon dioxide in the dark. The tree's supply of water comes from falling rain or lies buried as ground water. The rain comes from clouds that were formed from water vapor rising from oceans, rivers, and streams—some of the sources being far distant from the tree. The ground water, which feeds the tree's roots, is also part of the earth's water cycle, and the roots draw other forms of nourishment from below the earth's surface. The universal gravitational field anchors the tree on the earth, while the electromagnetic field is connected with the electrical activity in the tree's cells.

You could say that the whole universe supports this one little tree. Nothing can exist alone and isolated, but everything partakes in the being of all things. The Buddhist teacher Thich Nhat Hanh calls this connection among all things "interbeing."

Our Sense of Separateness

Although every being in the universe can exist only because of an intricate system of interconnections or "interbeing," at the present state of evolution of the human race, we tend to experience ourselves as isolated individuals. Our isolation is the result of identifying ourselves with our personality and its separative tendencies. We might think of ourselves in relation to our various principles as atma wearing a space suit to function in the world. The apparatus of this space suit at the level of the emotions and concrete mind is very sophisticated, resulting in our competency in the world of business and technology. But focusing on those outer levels tends to make us feel separated from other persons and confined within our own minds.

The suit works very well for its purpose, and we come to think of it as ourselves. But although it reveals the general shape of its wearer, it also conceals a great deal. We have to look through the window that covers the eyes to see the true individual. Atma is in there behind the physical, emotional, and mental apparatus, but atma is hard to find when covered over by the space suit.

Our Evolutionary Journey

In his studies of the human personality, C. G. Jung found that people who live in tribes have less independent thought and are more emotionally enmeshed in their group than those who live in more advanced social groups. For Jung, mature separation and a degree of independent individuality was a sign of growth. He called the process of becoming more independent "individuation." From the Theosophical perspective, we humans have the potential in our consciousness for both merging with the whole and maintaining relative independence, and we evolve from an *unconscious* oceanic state of oneness to a stage of relative separation and individualism, to a further stage of *conscious* merging.

Much of humanity has now passed the nadir of the separative tendency, and some are beginning to turn again toward a realization of oneness, but this time with mature realization of one's individuality. The practice of meditation in its many forms around the world today with an emphasis on unity, the overwhelming scientific evidence for interconnections, and an increasing recognition of the need for cooperation in every realm, including business and commerce, worldwide and locally, all bear witness to this growing realization. Though the tendency toward division and separation is still dominant, there are signs that a new consciousness is dawning.

The eventual goal of our sojourn in the many fields of being is to actualize their potentials in us, including our forgotten sense of unity. Blavatsky speaks of the *monad,* or atmic unit within us, as a "pilgrim" because it makes "an obligatory pilgrimage" or sacred journey through many kingdoms and levels of development. She defines *monad* as "that immortal part of man which reincarnates in the lower kingdoms and gradually progresses through them to Man and then to the final goal—Nirvana" (Blavatsky, *The Theosophical Glossary* 216). In the beginning, we humans are unitary consciousness with no sense of separation. Eventually, we become self-conscious, aware of ourselves as individuals. At the end of the journey, we are the same unitary consciousness but have become "individualized Self-Consciousness," in Blavatsky's words. This movement has been described as from unconscious perfection to conscious imperfection to conscious perfection.

A Mythic Journey

Myths and fairy tales about journeys depict this sojourn of our consciousness within the personality and body and its return home to atma. The story of Tom Thumb is one such tale.

Tom's father is a tailor and his mother spins thread. Tom, who was born prematurely, is no bigger than your thumb. Even though so small, he is eager to leave home and see the world. Among other adventures, Tom leads a horse drawing a cart by climbing into its ear and whispering to it. Tom collaborates with thieves by slipping between the bars of a window and handing money out to them. Later, he is swallowed by a cow that is fed hay in which Tom was sleeping. Tom's yelling inside the cow's stomach leads people to think the animal is possessed by evil spirits, so they slaughter her. But before Tom can escape from her stomach, he is swallowed by a wolf. Tom lures the wolf into his parents' kitchen by offering the wolf a meal if he will crawl through a drain. The wolf eats so much that he cannot fit into the drain to get out. Tom cries out in the wolf's stomach, and his father rescues him. His parents hug and kiss

Tom and give him food and drink and new clothes. His journey is over and he is happy to be home.

The story is a fantastic comedy on the literal level. But if we look at it from a cosmic point of view, Tom's parents can be seen as creating the form side of the universe. The thread his mother spins represents the substance from which the cosmos is woven. The fabric with which his father, the tailor, works is woven from the thread. Tom's parents suggest Brahman or God creating the form side of the cosmos.

Atma is described in the Upanishads as "greater than the great," that is, universal, but also "smaller than the small," a focus of pure Consciousness buried in the heart of every living being. Atma is unformed and inexperienced in the world, as Tom was when he was born prematurely. Tom is eager to leave home and see the world, as the pilgrim in each of us is eager to embark on a life of experience.

The cow is an earth symbol that can represent the physical body Tom takes on. The horse, too, is a symbol of the body, and Tom's guiding it represents taking control of the appetites. Tom's falling in with thieves and his being swallowed by a wolf symbolize greed and gluttony, aspects of human nature that Tom has to deal with. When he eventually finds his way home, he tells his father, "I've been about in the world a lot. Thank heaven I can breathe fresh air again." The literal meaning of *atma* is "breath." Tom has returned to the pure air of atma.

Atma Unfolding

Tom and we ourselves, as atma the pilgrim, unfold our inner latent powers as we journey through the many levels of experience. As Blavatsky put it, we ascend "through all the degrees of intelligence, from the lowest to the holiest archangel" (*Secret Doctrine* 1:17). Eventually, with our latent powers well developed, we reach the sacred goal of the pilgrimage, which is the realization of unity with the whole, not as unconscious sparks, but as fully Self-conscious individuals.

In the course of our journey, we gradually begin to realize who we really are. Attachments to purely personal concerns diminish, and we begin to sense the rich potentials of the higher mind, the intuition, and the spiritual will. We begin to take control of our personality and focus on the deeper realities of the transpersonal Self. We sense that the life of the Self is a richer, more satisfying way of being. Eventually we come to know ourselves as atma, limitless universal consciousness, empty and void in itself but able to function in us at any level.

Practices such as Yoga and meditation are designed to help us wake up to the reality of our true being in atma. They teach us to quiet the mind and find stillness at deep levels within. We slowly come to identify with that aspect of ourselves that is beyond the seemingly separate outer levels and rooted in the essence that permeates all. We come to sense unity within diversity, or as Blavatsky states, "from ONE light, seven lights" (*Secret Doctrine* 1:122). Atma is the true light of which all our various fields and powers are but luminous shadows, beautiful in themselves but only partial revelations of our essential being.

The Mystery of Consciousness

The Universe is nothing but Conscious, and in all its appearances reveals nothing but an evolution of Consciousness, from its origin to its end, which is a return to its cause. It is the goal of every "initiatory" religion to teach the way to this ultimate union.

R. S. Schwaller de Lubicz

As I sit in my yard among the late afternoon shadows, a baby cottontail peeks out from under a shrub. With nose wriggling up and down, she ventures into the open, pauses, sniffs some more, and begins to nibble blades of grass. A jay calls out raucously. The bunny scampers back under the shrub. After a few minutes she cautiously emerges and again nibbles. A crow caws. The bunny spins about and retreats into the bushes once more.

This baby is obviously conscious. Her behavior tells me that she is aware of sights and sounds around her and is reacting to them. My conscious experience of her tells me that she has conscious experiences, too. I cannot experience her consciousness directly. I am locked into my own world, and she has subjective, private experiences, known only to her. I cannot directly share her inner life, nor she mine. Yet both she and I can observe the conscious actions of others around us.

You have experienced consciousness vividly ever since you were born, and even before birth, while you were still in the womb. Except in dreamless sleep and abnormal unconscious states, you have continuous inner awareness of things around you and of your own sensations, thoughts, and feelings. This awareness is the ground of everything you experience, the background on which all experience arises. The table at which you sit feels solid and heavy, the sunflower in the garden looks yellow, the thrush's song drifting through the trees sounds melodious. But you know about these things only through your consciousness. That is how you can know anything at all, whether "out there" or within your own mind. If you are made unconscious by anesthesia or a blow or when you are in dreamless sleep, the outer and inner worlds cease to exist for you.

What Is Consciousness?

Consciousness has a protean quality. It can face outward to the moving traffic or inward to your sense of hurry and anxiety. It can expand to take in a panoramic view or contract to focus on a single tiny bud. It conforms to its changing contents. If your emotions are gloomy, you feel that your consciousness turns gloomy. If you are absorbed in plans for the summer, you experience consciousness as full of plans. If the temperature drops, your consciousness registers coldness. Changes in the contents of consciousness seem like changes in consciousness itself. But consciousness is the changeless background behind changing contents, the silent awareness within which all thoughts, emotions, and perceptions come and go.

Consciousness is a profound mystery that has baffled philoso-phers, psychologists, theologians, and ordinary people like you and me for centuries. Though consciousness is so intimate and familiar, it is difficult to identify. A dictionary may define the word as "a state of being characterized by sensation, emotion, volition, and thought." Varieties of consciousness listed in the dictionary—such as sentience, awareness, and reflection—have the common characteristic of sub-jectivity, of knowing from inside. They are what the Jesuit paleon-tologist Teilhard de Chardin called "the within of things" (53–74); they are what experience feels like from inside. They are the subjec-tivity that underlies all experience—the raw feel of awareness that is unmistakable.

In recent decades, an expanding field of inquiry into conscious-ness has grown up in areas such as cognitive science, neuroscience, social science, extrasensory perception, religious studies, and philos-ophy. Researchers have looked into such diverse areas as the brain and nervous system, contemplative practices, and quantum mechan-ics. The unbelievably complex functioning of the brain and its pharmacology have been probed by newly developed tools, and we now know many details about how the brain and nervous system function. The word "qualia" signifies subjective perceptions such as redness in an apple, pain from touching a hot grill, hunger pangs, as well as sensations of anger or grief or joy. But we have no idea what consciousness is or how an intention, an act in consciousness, can set up nervous and muscular impulses that cause an arm to raise or a head to turn. Various states of consciousness have been identi-fied and studied. But these as well as physical correlates to con-sciousness and changes in the contents of consciousness are not consciousness itself. Like electricity, which we know only by such means as meter readings, motors running, and bulbs lighting up, consciousness in itself defies definition. It remains a mystery.

You can easily observe the changing contents of your consciousness. Right now by a switch of attention you can notice a slight ache in your neck, your back beginning to tire, or the way this book feels in your hands. You can watch thoughts arise and pass away as you consider words on the page, perhaps evoking memories or related ideas. You may feel slight surges of emotion as approval or skepticism arises with thoughts. You can look through a window at a tree and perceive its image in your mind. At any time you can be aware of sensations, emotions, images, and thoughts moving through your stream of consciousness. But you are not aware of the ability to cognize all this, consciousness itself, which stands behind all the changing contents. Though it is always with us, consciousness is ordinarily imperceptible, as the eye that cannot see itself. Yet consciousness is the constant backdrop of all our experience, every moment throughout our whole lifetime. It is the changeless, colorless screen on which life's ever-changing moving pictures take place. We are well aware of the changing shadows but not of the screen on which they play, though we can get a fleeting glimpse of it in still moments between two thoughts.

Conscious and Unconscious

We feel that our consciousness is confined to what we are aware of at the moment and what we can easily recall. Yet we react to subliminal signals flashed for too short a time for them to register in awareness. Sigmund Freud and generations of psychologists and psychiatrists after him established that the full range of consciousness is far wider than our familiar waking consciousness. William James, a pioneer psychologist and member of the Theosophical Society, said, "Our normal waking consciousness is but one special type of consciousness, while all about it, parted from it by the filmiest of screens, there lie potential forms of consciousness entirely different. We may go through life without suspecting their existence, but apply the requisite stimulus and at a touch they are there in all their completeness."

These "potential forms of consciousness" include sensations, feelings, thoughts, and memories of which we are not aware. Freud himself had a dream in which the Latin name of a particular fern appeared. It turned out that there is such a fern with that name, but he was sure he had never seen or heard of it before. Yet some time later he found the Latin name written in his own hand in a notebook from his studies as a schoolboy. His consciousness somehow retained that distant memory, though it had vanished from his immediate awareness.

Using a metaphor that has become famous, Freud compared waking consciousness to the tip of an iceberg. He explored the "subconscious" beneath that tip, consisting, in his view, of lustful or hostile urges too threatening to be allowed into our awareness. C. G. Jung and others discovered higher, noble urges and wisdom of which we are normally unaware, deep in the "unconscious." Roberto Assiagoli, another psychotherapist, calls this area the "superconscious." He and other transpersonal psychologists deal with spiritual aspects of consciousness that are ordinarily beyond everyday awareness. We have memories, feelings, and thoughts that can easily be brought to awareness, sometimes called "preconscious," but there are also less accessible experiences buried in the deepest regions of the mind.

The contents of the subconscious and the superconscious are within a global consciousness that is larger than ordinary waking awareness. What we are aware of at a given moment is only a small part of our total consciousness. For example, you may have a dream that brings to mind a time when, as a child, you were in the hospital at Christmas time. Your feelings of being abandoned may arise with the memory of the incident. You were unaware that you had this memory until the dream evoked it. Yet, since it was retrievable, it was within the range of your wider consciousness.

How can we use the word *conscious* for something of which we are not conscious? Since *consciousness* implies awareness, perhaps we need another word for the range of potential inner experience. Blavatsky seemed to think so when she wrote, ". . . such is the poverty of language that we have no term to distinguish the knowledge not actively thought of from knowledge we are unable to recall to memory" (*Secret Doctrine* 1:56).

Not only memories but knowledge of transcendental truths are in our wider consciousness, though not our awareness. We know such things without knowing that we know them. In discussing absolute consciousness—undifferentiated consciousness without content—Blavatsky says, "This is not the kind of consciousness that we can manage to distinguish from what appears to us as unconscious" (*Secret Doctrine* 1:87).

Nonlocal Consciousness

Most of the time we feel encapsulated within our skins and minds, our "space suits." We are aware only of what the senses feed us at any given moment, plus any memories, thoughts, images, and feelings that arise inside us. But there is overwhelming evidence that consciousness can extend beyond the here and now and beyond what we have learned by means of the brain and senses. For example, it is not uncommon for someone to know of danger to, or the death of, a distant loved one.

In addition to such spontaneous incidents, there are thousands of controlled experiments on record showing that thoughts can be transferred from one person to another over distances. In one series of experiments, subjects were hooked to a device that measures electrodermal activity—an indication of the degree of activity in the autonomic nervous system, which controls functions like heartbeat and digestion. People with illnesses such as ulcers, high blood pressure, and anxiety neurosis have overactive autonomic functions. In the experiments, influencers tried to calm or stimulate autonomic activity in the patients, who were in another room by themselves. The influencers sent the patients mental imagery suitable to the mood they were trying to induce, sometimes themselves becoming calm or excited. Although the patients did not know when the thirty-second "influence" periods came, they consistently showed an increase in the intended direction during these periods. They sometimes reported getting images that matched the ones beamed at them. One subject reported a vivid impression of the influencer coming into his room, walking behind his chair, and shaking it vigorously. The influencer, trying to activate the subject from afar, had used just that image (Dossey, *Healing Words* 181).

Knowledge at a distance has been confirmed by years of controlled experiments in "remote viewing," underwritten by the United States government. In these experiments, typically one person drives to a distant spot, which he explores. While he is exploring, his partner in the lab tries to get in tune with him. She describes images that come into her mind while he is exploring. Judges report that these images match the place far more than would be expected by chance. The researchers believe that everyone has latent ability to sense something at a distance (Murphy 279–82). "Nonlocality" is a term borrowed from quantum physics to describe this ability of consciousness to extend beyond the immediate locality of the person who is conscious. It has also been referred to as "field consciousness," a term that suggests a continuum of consciousness in which space is no impediment.

Consciousness and Matter

There is reason to believe that consciousness is not just a byproduct of the intricate arrangement of complex molecules in the brain, as materialistic science has traditionally held. Theosophy teaches, and some contemporary scientists concur, that the entire universe is conscious, that even apparently inert minerals have some degree of sensitivity or sentience. The biologist and Nobel laureate George Wald concluded, with some of the "monumental physicists" who first explored the contemporary realm of subatomic particles, that some type of mind or consciousness is in all matter, so that mind and matter are twin aspects of reality. According to Wald, "One has no more reason to ask that matter occur without some aspect of mind accompanying it than to ask for radiation that is waves and not simultaneously particles" (43).

Teilhard de Chardin held that there is an inner, conscious side to everything, animate and inanimate, "the within of things." He argued that any phenomenon that exists in a highly developed form in nature must exist in a rudimentary way throughout nature. "It is impossible to deny that, deep within ourselves, an 'interior' appears at the heart of beings, as if it were seen through a rent. This is enough to ensure that, in one degree or another, this 'interior' should obtrude itself as existing everywhere in nature from all time" (56). Thus, he argues, consciousness, which is highly developed and apparent in human beings, must exist in some rudimentary form, even in mineral matter. Wald concurs: "The whole cosmos, if it is to produce consciousness in creatures like us, must be of the nature of consciousness beforehand" (44).

Teilhard's and Wald's view is exactly the Theosophical one. According to Blavatsky, "Everything in the Universe, throughout all its kingdoms, is conscious: i.e., endowed with a consciousness of its own kind and on its own plane of perception. We men must remember that, simply because *we* do not perceive any signs which we can recognize—of consciousness—say, in stones, we have no right to say that *no consciousness exists there*. There is no such thing as either 'dead' or 'blind' matter" (*Secret Doctrine* 1:274). The root of consciousness is always present with matter. Transpersonalists like the psychiatrist John Nelson concur that consciousness is nonphysical and interacts with matter everywhere. According to the psychologist Gardner Murphy, this does not disparage the flowering of consciousness in humans but rather glorifies the primal ooze from which life arose.

Undivided Consciousness

Ordinarily, we experience ourselves as separate and apart from the whole of things. But according to John Nelson, "The ordinary state of consciousness is neither innate nor normal but simply one specialized tool for coping with the ordinary environment and people" (15). At the level of pure consciousness, behind the changing contents, we are one with everything, a focus of that which is undivided and universal. The seemingly separate self is an illusion. The philosopher Carlos Suares holds that in consciousness there can be no compartments, no partitions or dividing walls. Without our concepts of who we are, what groups we belong to, and what our roles are as opposed to the roles of others, there are no divisions. Blavatsky tells us that "Consciousness (as such) is ubiquitous and can neither be localized nor centered in any particular subject, nor can it be limited" (*Secret Doctrine* 1:387). One pervasive consciousness runs through us and everything else. As numberless ponds and even muddy puddles reflect the one moon, the light of consciousness in each of us has but one source. Those who have experienced this consciousness in its purity tell us that, in spite of outer distinctions, inwardly we are all one. The Indian sage Ramana Maharshi says that in the transcendental awareness where there is Being alone, "There is no you, no I, no he" (Wilber, *Sex, Ecology, Spirituality* 314). As the mystic poet Rumi put it, "I, you, he, she, we, / In the garden of mystic lovers / These are not true distinctions" (Moyers 57).

Our consciousness is not really "our" consciousness at all, but rather is universally shared. Our ordinary experience of consciousness is a pale reflection of atma, modified and stepped down through our principles and the vehicles in which consciousness works. Lama Govinda, deep student of Tibetan Buddhism, commenting on the Lankavatara Sutra, says that intellectual consciousness (concrete mind) sorts and judges sense impressions, followed by attractions and repulsions. "Universal consciousness," on the other hand, "is compared to the ocean, on the surface of which currents, waves, and whirlpools are formed, while its depths remain motionless, unperturbed, pure, and clear" (Govinda, *Foundations of Tibetan Mysticism* 73–74). Mind is the focal point between surface and depth consciousness. Atma, the one infinite consciousness, is focused in us as individuals.

Consciousness, the Creator

The fundamental Reality from which the universe arises is called *Parabrahm* in Indian philosophy. Like the original fireball posited by the Big Bang theory, the potential for everything that unfolds throughout time inheres in it. We cannot fathom its nature, but the Upanishads and other traditional sources characterize it as Consciousness. The Brihadaranyaka Upanishad says, ". . . the supreme Spirit is an ocean of pure consciousness boundless and infinite" (Mascaro 132). Blavatsky refers to the One Reality as "the field of Absolute Consciousness" (*Secret Doctrine*, 1:15).

Consciousness creates the world in which we live. You can see this in your everyday sense experience. For example, you look at a sunflower and perceive its petals as bright yellow. But what has happened, objectively speaking? Light of 590 millimicron wavelength has bounced into your eyes and stimulated your nervous system. Your brain responded to the stimulus, and you saw yellow. But there is no yellow in your retina or in the electrical and chemical events in your brain. Nor does yellow exist in the wavelength associated with it. Your consciousness somehow superimposes the experience of yellow onto these events.

We do not see "the thing in itself," as philosophers put it. Perception of reality requires a transmitter from the external world and a subject as receiver. All individual receivers create their own pictures of reality; we each create our own world, depending on our unique inner filters and our state of consciousness at the moment. We see only what comes through, and that is colored by our sense organs and also by our minds. Indeed, the way we perceive the world is heavily influenced by our worldview, attitudes, expectations, ideas, and preconceptions, as well as by our physical organs. As Lama Anagarike Govinda says, "Our consciousness . . . by its selective faculties of perception and co-ordination determines the type of world in which we live. A different kind of consciousness would create a different world around us, whatever the . . . raw material of the universe may be" (*Way of the White Clouds* 123).

According to Theosophy, just as we create our private world through consciousness, so the whole of the manifested universe is brought into being by Universal Consciousness, the subjective side of the universal process, called atma or Brahman or God. As the Indian sage Shankaracharya asserted, Brahman is Absolute Consciousness. This view of consciousness as a fundamental attribute of the divine is taught, not only by Eastern philosophers, but also by Christian mystics such as Meister Eckhart, by Pythagorean and Platonic philosophers, and even by some scientific theorists. As the ancient Hermetic principle states, the world works "from within without," from the inner domain of pure atma or consciousness to the dense material world. Consciousness precedes all forms and indeed calls forth forms into being as vehicles for its expression. It conceives, constructs, and subsequently governs visible matter. As

George Wald declares, "Mind or consciousness is a constant pervasive presence guiding matter" (43).

Quantum Physics and Consciousness

Some quantum physicists are finding corroboration for this ancient view of the primacy of consciousness. For example, Amit Goswami, a physicist and former researcher for the Institute of Noetic Science, finds in the behavior of quanta support for the view of consciousness as universal and impartible. Quanta are discrete bits of energy emitted by objects such as electrons and photons. These unimaginably small bits of matter and energy do strange things that defy Newtonian physics and common sense. For example, electrons instantaneously jump from one orbit around the nucleus of an atom to another orbit, without traversing the space between. Further defying Newtonian physics, unless they are observed and measured, subatomic particles spread out and exist as probability waves in more than one place. They show up in diffraction pictures as fuzzy orbits or clouds. Electrons can pass through two slits at the same time. But when measured by tracking them in a cloud chamber, they always appear in a single place, as particles. The conscious act of observing them brings them from a cloud of uncertainty into space-time reality as particles. Somehow consciousness and the choice of an experiment select whether they appear as a particle or a wave.

Furthermore, if two electrons or photons interact for a period of time and then are separated, even by a great distance, they still affect each other. For example, measuring one and collapsing it from a wave to a particle state simultaneously collapses the other one. Such instantaneous influence without any signals in space-time is called "nonlocality." Some physicists recognize that the two quanta objects are connected in a transcendent domain, out of space-time, where the probability waves of quantum physics exist. The physicist

Henry Stapp finds reason to believe that "the fundamental process of Nature lies outside space-time but generates events that can be located in space-time" (Goswami, *Self-Aware Universe* 61).

Goswami makes a case for this transcendent domain as nonlocal consciousness. He espouses "monistic idealism," the view that consciousness, not matter, is primary and is the ground of being. He points out that both material objects, such as balls, and mental objects, such as the thought of balls, are known only by means of consciousness. We never experience a material object without an associated mental object, so material objects and mental objects are both objects of consciousness. Goswami quotes C. G. Jung as saying it is "probable that psyche [subjective experience] and matter are two different aspects of one and the same thing" (127).

According to monistic idealism, our consciousness, as the subject that experiences an object like a ball, is the same consciousness that is the ground of being. But we do not recognize our familiar waking consciousness, in which we feel separate and discrete, as this universal consciousness, which transcends space and time and is all-pervading, not limited to what we can see or know about locally. Writer and Theosophist Norman Hankin explains how we can experience the ultimate Ground: "The path through human consciousness . . . can be opened by ourselves by simply retreating from particular objects and centering ourselves in our ground consciousness, in that proper 'being-as-consciousness' which is what we as selves are. . . . When we withdraw our gaze from . . . items in the 'foreground' and refocus in (not on) their background . . . then we experience being in the interface of ourselves and the ultimate Ground" (137).

Self-Consciousness

Although consciousness occurs in everything that is, only in the human kingdom do we find self-consciousness. You have known for as long as you can remember that you are different from your brother, from your car, from the plants in your garden. You may wake up in a strange place and wonder: Where am I? But you never wonder: Who am I? You have had a sense of being a self—yourself—that (except for cases of severe amnesia) stays with you through profound changes as you grow older through all the seasons of life. You have a persistent sense of I-am-ness, of egoship, of being yourself and no one else. As Annie Besant says, "The Self is that conscious, feeling, ever-existing one that in each of us knows himself as existing" (*Thought Power* 13).

Yet we have not always had this seemingly inborn sense. Newborn babies have to learn to differentiate between themselves and what is around them. Somewhat older babies look at one of their hands or feet, seeming to wonder what that strange object is. When they are a little older their sense of self includes their body parts, and they know that their body is part of themselves.

Researcher John Broughton has mapped the developmental stages of knowing oneself, of self-consciousness (Wilber, *Sex, Ecology, Spirituality* 268–70). He asked individuals from preschool age to early adulthood, "What or where is your *self?*" He found that toddlers feel that the self is "inside" and reality is "outside." Slightly older children believe that the self is identified with the physical body, but the mind controls the self and can tell it what to do: the mind is a big person and the body is a little person. At ages seven to twelve, the self is not a body but a *person*, a social role that includes both mind and body. At ages eleven to seventeen, the social personality or role is seen as a false outer appearance, different from the true inner self. These young people begin to glimpse the self as the nature that remains itself amid changes in mental contents. Reflective self-awareness dawns, so that they can entertain thoughts and feelings independent of the social situation. At later stages, the self as observer is distinguished from the ideas we have about who we are, or our self-concept.

Adults at the highest levels of development identify with an observing self or witness as distinguished from the outer, objective self or persona. They no longer think of themselves exclusively as the body, persona, ego, and mind, but they can integrate these in a unified fashion. Over many years, the sense of self evolves from simply differentiating oneself from the environment to identifying with the awareness or consciousness that stands behind the changing elements that make up the objective self (Wilber, *Sex, Ecology, Spirituality* 260–62).

Animals may have a rudimentary sense of self-consciousness, but they probably cannot differentiate themselves from their appetites, instincts, and actions. Dolphins can be trained to modify their behavior, but can they examine their motivation or replay and evaluate an incident? Can they address their own mind and its content or stand back from these and identify with the consciousness through which they know anything?

Since self-consciousness is apparently a human characteristic, it is surprising that Blavatsky says, "Every atom in the Universe has the potentiality of self-consciousness in it" (*Secret Doctrine* 1:107). This is a powerful statement of her conviction that consciousness exists in varying forms everywhere, not only as we know it. She also says that there is no potentiality for self-consciousness in pure spirit or consciousness: "It is only through a vehicle of matter that consciousness wells up as 'I am I'" (1:15). Pure consciousness or atma must become involved in the principles and the vehicles of matter before a sense of self as opposed to other can arise.

The Subject-Object Split

Blavatsky links self-consciousness with mind or *manas,* which is the hallmark of human beings. One function of the mind is to separate and divide, to classify things into compartments. This ability creates order from the confusion of the many sense impressions that impinge on our minds. But in this process of differentiating and pigeonholing, without especially meaning to do so, we divide the world into two basic categories—myself and everything else. Ordinarily, we experience ourselves as a subject who is aware of objects. Even our own thoughts and feelings appear as objective to the subject who is ourselves.

This subject-object split pervades our experience most of the time. We set ourselves, as observer, apart from any contents that arise in our consciousness. This setting-apart leads to experiencing ourselves as separate and alienated from everything else. Yet both the subject we identify with and the objects we observe occur in one consciousness that has become polarized into subject and object. Both of these vanish in the light of atma, the ground consciousness behind them, which has been described as a boundless field of awareness with no subject, no object. Blavatsky says, "Absolute Consciousness contains the cognizer, the thing cognized and the cognition, all three in itself and all three *one*" (*Secret Doctirne* 1:56).

The mind conceives of the subjective "I" as an entity with continuity. It appears to us that we are an ongoing, definite self apart from everything else. But a deep awareness of inner processes reveals that this sense of self comes from stringing memories together. As many meditation masters have discovered, our usual sense of an independent "I" is an illusion, a crystallized concept in our minds. Observing the contents of the mind reveals only passing sensations, thoughts, emotions, memories, and images, with no self encapsulated anywhere in them. What we usually think of as "I" is a reference point that orients us in the rushing stream of changing contents of consciousness. The twentieth-century sage, Ramana Maharshi, says, "Since the Self, which is pure Consciousness, cognizes everything, it is the Ultimate Seer. . . . All the rest: ego, mind, body, etc., are merely its objects; so each one of them except the Self or pure Consciousness is a merely externalized object and cannot be the true Seer" (Wilber, *Spectrum of Consciousness* 71). If we learn to extricate ourselves from the changing stream of the contents of consciousness, we can truly know who we are.

What we take to be a separate, individualized ego that plans and chooses is a secondary entity. It is a localization in time and space of pure, undivided cosmic consciousness. Amit Goswami says it is brought into being by an individual brain-mind and its belief that it *is* the body-mind. He and other physicists such as Erwin Schroedinger hold that the subject of experience is a single universal subject for everyone, not our personal ego. Schroedinger said, "Consciousness is a singular for which there is no plural." Fundamentally, our consciousness is consciousness of Being or, one could say, of God—transcendent, out of time and space, beyond the subject-object split. Goswami says that consciousness has no other source, for it is all there is. In other words, atma and Brahman are one, or as said by the German mystic Meister Eckhart speaking of his mystical apprehension, "I receive an impulse which shall bring me above all the angels . . . In this breakthrough I discover that I and God are one" (Wilber, *Sex, Ecology, Spirituality* 311).

Yet at a level deeper than our tendency for egotistical self-centeredness, there is an immortal center of being in us, our localization in the universal field of atma. Atma is the most difficult of the principles to understand because it is both a localized center of consciousness in a human being *(jivatma)* and a continuous field of consciousness. As the immortal center of each individual, it takes on a vehicle of *buddhi,* the most ethereal of the principles or fields. This combination of atma and buddhi is called the "monad" by Blavatsky. It is "the immortal part of man which reincarnates," also called "the Unity, the One," but also means "the duad, atma-Buddhi" (*The Theosophical Glossary* 216). It is the "pilgrim," our permanent locus of consciousness throughout our long evolutionary journey in the fields. Our fundamental sense of being a self is a reflection of this abiding focus of consciousness.

Yet, though atma-buddhi in each of us is individual, it is not separate from universal consciousness, the One Life. Blavatsky says it is "the egotistical . . . principle in man, due to our ignorance which separates our 'I' from the Universal One-Self" (*Theosophical Glossary* 10).

As the above discussion shows, the word "self" can be used in various ways. Here "self" signifies the personality; that is, the physical body, emotions, and concrete or lower mind. The philosophical or higher mind, intuition, and spiritual will is called the "transpersonal Self," as explained earlier. Atma as Brahman, the continuous field of consciousness or ultimate Ground of Being, is designated as "Self" or "One Self."

Self and Symbols

Our ability to observe what goes on within us makes it possible for us to think abstractly and to use symbols, which are principally human characteristics. By stepping outside our experience, we can give names and symbols to the things we have experienced and mentally map them. The psychologist Rollo May states that "the capacity to transcend the immediate situation is the basic and unique characteristic of human existence" (May, Angel, and Ellenberger, *Existence* 75). This capacity is the result self-awareness: "The mere awareness of oneself as a being in the world implies the capacity to stand outside and look at one's self and the situation and to assess and guide one's self by an infinite variety of possibilities" (74).

You can study the symbols on a map and decide on the best route to your vacation hideaway. You can imagine the experiences you would have if you choose one college or one career instead of another. You can be guided by the pros and cons of any decision you have to make. This ability to transcend the situation enhances our power to control our lives and thus enhances our sense of self, as we experience ourselves as a center of choice and of action. The use of computers has revolutionized our ability to foresee the results of various decisions, as we study computer models of the outcomes of ideas before they are put into practice.

Consciousness and the Principles

Our ordinary experience does not tell us that we are part of universal Consciousness, one with the divine. We feel confined within our body, mind, and emotions, with which we usually identify ourselves, because our principles and their various vehicles or fields heavily color our conscious experience. As explained before, we do not experience pure consciousness in itself but only its contents mixed with the characteristics of the principles. As Annie Besant points out, "Mind unconsciously modifies what it sees as though through colored glasses and presents a combination of itself and the object perceived" (*Thought Power* 26).

The principles are aspects of the one undivided consciousness, as electricity and magnetism are aspects of the one electromagnetic field. Electricity can produce many effects. Plug in your toaster, and its filaments glow with heat. Turn on your stereo, and sound fills the air. Flip the switch on your wall, and your room lights up. One electrical force produces those very different effects, depending on the machinery it operates through. Similarly, consciousness operates in many modes, depending on the particular principles it is energizing.

Consciousness working through the mental field as manas wells up as mind-consciousness or mental cognition. Consciousness working through the emotional field wells up as emotions such as anger or excitement or boredom. Emotion is the instrument by which we as the knower vividly experience our inner and outer worlds. Both mind and emotion are instruments used to obtain knowledge. All the principles and their sheaths are the means by which the supreme consciousness is brought under the spell of a seemingly separate personal self.

Mental, emotional, and other differentiations within the one consciousness are atma's latent potentials, which embodied life draws out into active powers. Our ability to cognize, to remember, to use logic, to visualize, to plan ahead; flashes of sudden comprehension or creativity; our capacity to feel love and hate, elation and despair, excitement and boredom; even our physical perceptions such as of hot and cold—all these and more are powers inherent in our principles. The principles reveal the orderly structure latent in atma, just as the colors of the rainbow are latent in clear light. Blavatsky describes the principles as "seven individual and fundamental aspects of the One Universal Reality in Kosmos and in man" (*Theosophical Glossary* 262). Elsewhere she says, "We divide man into seven principles. . . . These principles are all aspects of one principle, and even this principle is but a temporary and periodical ray of the One eternal and infinite Flame or Fire" (*Collected Writings* 10:335). We can think of the principles and powers as luminous shadows that reveal something of the light of atma while concealing its fullness.

These seven differentiations as planes and principles operate throughout the cosmos, not only in us humans. As physicists posit a unified field encompassing all known physical fields, atma, the One Life, Brahman, God can be thought of as a unified field in which all the principles, fields, and levels of the cosmos inhere. We are each a microcosm of the great macrocosm, according to Theosophy and other wisdom traditions; the structure of our nature mirrors that of the universe. The cosmos itself has fields or spheres of mentality and emotionality that are evoked by living beings. Not only consciousness but sentience and intelligence exist everywhere. We can see sentience in plants as they react to light, and intelligence working in them as they unconsciously unfold geometric patterns in their flowers. Animals display intelligence and emotion as they protect their young. Thus, each of us, far from being separate and independent, has our being in a system of interpenetrating universal fields at different levels. We are supported by and are part of the entire cosmos.

Our Vehicles, Sheaths, or Fields

Blavatsky explains that atma in itself cannot be effective in the world without a material vehicle in which to manifest itself. But she is not referring to physical matter only. Each of the human principles is an expression of a universal field or "plane," a term used by Blavatsky and other earlier Theosophical writers. These fields interpenetrate each other. They are intermediate states that range from the filmiest supersensual buddhic to the dense physical world.

Each level is characterized by its own unique kind of matter. *The Secret Doctrine* (1:139) says, "Just as a human being is composed of seven principles, differentiated matter in the solar system exists in seven different conditions." There are seven such levels that correspond to the seven human principles such as the physical, vital, and emotional. The matter in all except the physical is too rarefied for our senses to register, but it is still matter. The matter of the emotional level is sometimes referred to as "astral" matter because of its luminous or "starry" quality. Matter at the mental level is called "mental" matter, though it, too, is luminous.

The vehicles through which atma operates in physical and superphysical matter are sometimes called "bodies" or, in the Indian tradition, "sheaths." Blavatsky's descriptions, and much more the Indian ones, were written before the development of field theory in physics. Today the principles and their vehicles and the "planes" that support them are often described as fields. In physics, a field is a region in space in which an energy, such as magnetism, acts in an organizing way upon physical matter. Similarly, each nonmaterial principle organizes the superphysical matter associated with it.

You probably experienced the seemingly miraculous action of a field in elementary school. You were given a bar magnet to explore and play with. You discovered that if you point one end (the negative pole) toward bits of iron, the bits race over empty space to clamp onto the magnet. If you point the other end (the positive pole), the iron bits spring away from the magnet. A Laplander, who lectured in Atlanta, Georgia, in the 1940s, described how Laplanders hunted with the help of magnetism. Subsisting on reindeer through the long Arctic nights, they would look up at the aurora borealis, that tenuous aura of light and color caused by conditions in the earth's magnetic field. The deer pawed the snow looking for moss, striking magnetic stones underneath, which disturbed the magnetic field. The disturbance appeared as ripples in the aura borealis, a giveaway of the deer's location!

Just as a magnet affects the position of iron bits around it or magnetic changes on the ground affect the aurora borealis, so similarly consciousness affects the fields associated with the human principles. At one moment you might stir up the emotional field by powerful surges of feeling. At another time you might stimulate the mental field by concentrated thought. You bring buddhi or the intuitive field into life from time to time as you catch glimmerings from the domain of unlearned knowledge or you sense oneness. Sometimes you can evoke the will aspect of atma as you make life decisions and commitments. When our consciousness becomes active in these fields, our principles also become active at various levels. Consciousness expresses itself in the world through these vehicles of matter—shadows of itself.

All the fields interpenetrate one another, just as the electromagnetic and gravitational fields do; our principles are interdependent and inseparable in manifestation. This interdependence is borne out by the work of health professionals like Bernie Siegel, Joan Borysenko, and Larry Dossey, who have shown that health involves not only the physical level but mental, emotional, and spiritual levels as well. You can see for yourself that every thought, even if abstract, touches off some degree of emotion, and every emotion that arises is accompanied by at least some degree of thought. Thought and feeling are so closely related that we really "feel-think" or "flink," as it has been put humorously. We cannot modify one of our principles without also changing the others in some measure. Even at the higher levels, as will be seen in later chapters, the will is intertwined with desire, and the intuition or buddhi is reflected in emotions.

The Aura

We are normally not aware of the sphere of luminous matter called the "aura," in which each of us exists. The aura is composed of matter at the emotional and mental levels of our consciousness. This matter changes in response to whatever we are experiencing at the moment. When you feel a rush of affection for your child, it glows pink. When you get angry at your computer, lurid red appears. Think strongly of someone, and a picture of her face may appear at the mental level of your aura. Or contemplate the beauty and order behind all life, and a symmetrical mandala-like figure appears. Clairvoyants with paranormal vision perceive such effects in the aura, though projections and distortions are common in most clairvoyance.

According to many clairvoyant descriptions, the aura is seen as shining lights that constantly move and change. In her book *The Personal Aura*, Dora Kunz says, "To me the higher dimensions are forms of radiant energy related to light. . . . Clairvoyance may be an instrument which makes some otherwise invisible wavelengths and frequencies come within the range of perception" (14). The emotional or astral levels of our being are literally luminous—reflections of the atma in moving light. As mentioned, *astral* means "starry." Higher levels may also be experienced as light, appearing luminescent to clairvoyant vision. Even the physical body has a counterpart in subtler matter, the vital body as it is called, which is the medium through which the universal energy of prana enlivens the physical body (chapter 3).

Conditioning of Our Vehicles

We rarely experience pure consciousness in itself because, as explained, our emotional, mental, and other fields so strongly affect what we experience. In addition, the vehicles easily take on habits and conditioning and automatically repeat whatever we practice. You can brush your teeth, type a letter, or drive a car without telling your body what to do. It automatically repeats a familiar action. In the same way, emotions and thoughts repeat on their own. Thoughts of loved ones come up unbidden, as does worry about paying bills, or annoyance when a salesperson phones during dinner. No one wants to feel depression, but it pops up by itself from time to time. Repetitive thoughts and attitudes like disapproval or criticism intrude, though you may want to be loving and accepting. Nietzsche complained that a thought would come to him as it will, not as he willed. William James said that, rather than saying "I think," one should say "thought goes on."

Instances of automatic action like those described in the preceding paragraph show that the vehicles have a kind of semiconscious life of their own that is not necessarily in harmony with you as their central consciousness. Your body wants to indulge in a second helping of ice cream, though *you* want to lose weight. Your emotions want you to stay up late watching a scary movie on television, though *you* want to get enough rest and be alert for work the next morning. Such conflicts are brought to life in the young Jiddu Krishnamurti's short treatise *At the Feet of the Master,* which advises us to learn to differentiate between ourselves as the consciousness and the various fields we inhabit. We do not see things in the light of pure consciousness but rather through the coloration of the fields and their conditioning. The conditioning is a property of the fields or sheaths, not of the consciousness that inhabits them.

Consciousness without Content

The aging Joseph Campbell was able to see himself as consciousness. In a television conversation, Bill Moyers asked Campbell how he felt about old age and dying. Campbell said he wasn't upset by his body deteriorating. Then he asked rhetorically, "Am I the bulb or the light?" He knew himself as consciousness, not its vehicle. Spiritual insight leads to detachment from the contents of consciousness—our thoughts, opinions, emotions, attitudes, roles, status, sensations, and body. And it leads to a realization of ourselves as atma, the consciousness in which all the contents arise. Thoreau saw himself as consciousness, the witness outside the stream of thoughts and actions. He wrote that he was conscious of a part of himself that yet was not a part of himself but a spectator that noted his experience but did not take part in it. This "spectator," he felt, was no more himself than any other person.

Imagine being in an isolation tank. You are floating in warm water that is the same temperature as your body. You cannot see anything because your eyes are covered, and "white noise" is fed into your ears. There are no sensations for you to focus on. In addition to this sensory deprivation, you have managed to calm your emotions so that they are quiet, and your mind has stopped churning up its usual stream of thoughts. All familiar experiences are stilled. What would you experience in such a state? Only pure consciousness without content, bare awareness in itself. You would not be distracted by your principles and their vehicles but would be thrown back to primordial consciousness, simply the ability to cognize or know.

Ordinarily, people cannot bear sensory deprivation for long. Subjects studied in isolation tanks begin to hallucinate and thus give content to their empty consciousness. But for a meditator who gradually develops a mind that can release all content, an experience of this emptiness is considered a high state of meditation in some systems. A taste of it helps us disentangle ourselves from the hooks of our minds, emotions, and bodies.

The Buddha made it clear that suffering comes from clinging to life and to our notions about ourselves. A glimpse of emptiness momentarily frees us from the roles, attitudes, goals, and emotions that we ordinarily identify with. Such glimpses begin to loosen our hold on our idea of who we are, and we see ourselves as something different from the changing conditions in which we usually live. At such moments we drop our worries and concerns, detach from our roles in life, and rest in simple being. When we can momentarily shake free from our vehicles and their conditioning, we can hold life more lightly and let in more joy.

Training is needed to accomplish this disidentification. We need to train our personal mind so that it is not so much engrossed in self-centered thoughts. We can do so because as humans we have self-consciousness and can observe our thoughts and emotions objectively. By cultivating the standpoint of the witness, we can come to use the powers of our principles and vehicles rather than being used by them. We override their semiconscious life, and they become instruments on which we as consciousness play, as the pianist plays on piano keys. The keys can make their own sounds, but only the musician playing on them can make music. I. K. Taimni says a goal of spiritual training is "wielding with perfect mastery the powers and faculties belonging to all the planes in carrying out the divine Will" (*Way of Self-Discovery* 41).

Deep listening is also a way to experience pure consciousness beyond the duality of subject and object—of me as opposed to something else. Jean Klein writes, "When you listen without being aggressive or resisting, your whole body becomes this listening, it is not confined to the ears. Everything surrounding you is included in this global listening and ultimately there is no longer a listener and something listened to. You are then on the threshold of non-duality" (52).

Consciousness and Evolution

Theosophy teaches that through life experiences—both happy and tragic—we are unfolding the potentials of atma through our principles. We, as the human species, develop ever more refined powers of mind, emotion, intuition, and will. We are also penetrating into superconscious realms of experience beyond the personality. We are broadening our boundaries and thus enlarging our sense of self. We are evolving toward the goal of conscious unity with all.

Meditations and spiritual practices can help move us toward that goal as they purify the mind and remove obstructions to the spontaneous revelation of atma. Teachers like Jiddu Krishnamurti and Ramana Maharshi emphasize the importance of achieving an unobstructed consciousness, in which all our experience, even awareness of the superconscious, takes place. When we achieve that goal, we will know that the consciousness we experience is one in its nature with universal consciousness. Father Bede Griffith, a Catholic priest who founded an ashram in India, understood the universality of consciousness when he wrote:

> We are slowly recovering . . . the knowledge which was universal in the ancient world, that there is no such thing as matter apart from mind or consciousness. Consciousness is latent in every particle of matter and the mathematical order which science discovers in the universe is due to the working of the universal consciousness in it. In human nature this latent consciousness begins to come into actual consciousness, and as human consciousness develops it grows more and more conscious of the universal consciousness in which it is grounded. (Anderson 27)

We, ourselves, are fundamentally no other than that primal consciousness at the base of all that is: atma. Our deepest, pure, unqualified consciousness, free of any content, is one with universal consciousness. Seers and sages testify that, by stripping away all objects from consciousness, it is possible to experience this most basic Self, our primary consciousness. As Shankaracharya says in *The Crest Jewel of Wisdom*, "The wise man is one who understands that the essence of Brahman and Atman is Pure Consciousness, and who realizes their absolute identity." Or in the words of Annie Besant, "The SELF of the universe and the SELF of man are one, and in knowing the SELF we know That which is at the root of the universe and of man alike" (*Self and Its Sheaths* 5).

Chapter 3

The Body: Our Physical and Energetic Instrument

The body has to submit to a mutation and be no longer the clamorous animal or the impeding clod it now is, but become instead a conscious servant and radiant instrument and living form of the spirit.

Lama Anagarika Govinda

Dr. Barker puts his hand on Jenny's flushed brow, noticing its sweatiness and the red spots on her chest and arms. He takes her pulse and listens to her breathing. He looks in her ears and eyes, palpitates her abdomen, and listens to her lungs with his stethoscope. He asks the child's mother about symptoms and the course of the illness. But he already knows what is wrong. He "smells" the measles, mostly from his physical examination. He smiles at the child and mother, reassuring them that Jenny will be all right. He writes out a prescription for something to make the little girl more comfortable.

John Barker is a physician in family practice. He is relaxed and easy-going with his patients and has a gift for sensing what is wrong when they visit him. He listens to what they say but relies on examinations to guide him, attending carefully to such tangible factors as heart rate, breathing, and pallor or flush, though he does not hesitate to order tests when he thinks they are needed. He remembers details about his patients' case histories and the way they usually look. He likes to depend on physical evidence more than inferences in making diagnoses.

Dr. Barker is realistic about his patients' lifestyle and the impact illness will have on the family. He often comes up with practical solutions for their problems. He is warm but matter-of-fact and practical with his patients. His skills have come more from his own experience than from theories and from reading.

John is good with machinery. His wife relies on him to fix things that break, and he likes to putter with the motor of his car. He taught his ten-year-old son the principles of auto mechanics. John enjoys playing basketball with his son, and he works out regularly at a local gym as well as runs several times a week. His wife likes to write poetry using symbols to capture feelings and ideas, but John does not enjoy her poems. He likes reading stories and articles that are heavy with descriptive detail. He collects pottery with unusual glazes and displays the pieces in a glass cabinet, though he lets his wife use them for serving or for flower arrangements. He enjoys his home, his car, and good clothes, as well as delicious food.

John would be classified as sensory and extravert on the Myers-Briggs Personality Inventory. This test reveals whether a person looks at the world more through sensation, emotion, thinking, or intuition, as well as whether the person is primarily turned inward (introvert) or focused on others (extravert). Those who are primarily sense-oriented are anchored in solid facts, not in ideas or speculation, and tend to build wholes from small pieces. They are good observers and perceive details that other types might miss. Because of their attention to detail, they sense life in an intensely individual way. They never fight the facts and pride themselves on being realistic. They are consistent and tend to be stable and enjoy routine. Sense-oriented people are found in such fields as mechanical engineering, machine operation, sales of clothing or physical merchandise, gardening, and design. Knowing something about the way these people relate to life through the body and senses helps us understand the physical principle.

The Senses and Consciousness

The senses on which sensory extraverts rely so heavily are our main way of contacting the world outside ourselves. We have learned a great deal through science about how the senses work. Impressions received through the eyes, ears, and other sense organs stimulate the nerves and send electrical and chemical messages to specific areas of the brain. But there science stops. How activity in the nervous system and brain becomes translated into the conscious experience of vision, hearing, or smelling remains a mystery.

Another mystery is the way we integrate impressions from different sensations. Somehow the brain melds shiny red color, smooth texture, sweet taste, and piquant aroma to give the experience of an apple. Various areas of the brain are involved in this perception, but how it is translated into conscious experience is not understood. Furthermore, we do not perceive the apple within our skull where the impressions occur. We project it out in front of us so accurately that we can pick up the apple precisely where it is. Consciousness creates the world we experience. The Buddha said that within this physical body lies the world and the rising of the world and the ceasing of the world.

Sensing and perceiving are far from simple, mechanical processes. There are many factors—in the sense organs, the nerves, and the brain—that can lead to false perceptions and misreading of the world around us. In addition, our preconceptions and attitudes can also distort what we think we sense; perceptions are heavily colored by our attitudes, expectations, memories, and conditioning from the past. For example, you see a small yellow-and-black striped insect flying nearby. You are allergic to bees and know that if you are stung you will have severe reactions. Fear arises and you hurry inside. However, what you perceived as a dangerous bee is really a relatively harmless yellow jacket. But your sensory mechanism interprets it according to your previous frightening experience of bees.

Some distortions enhance perception rather than mislead it, as several examples show (Murphy 65–6). Helen Keller, who was blind and deaf, could detect a coming storm through her sense of smell. As the storm drew near, her nostrils dilated. Then she would receive a "flood of earth odors that seem to multiply and extend, until I feel the splash of rain against my cheek." Bushmen in the Kalahari desert hear approaching animals, even in their sleep, by lying with an ear to the ground. Athletes sometimes report enhanced perception when they are participating in a game. Paul Martha, the former safety on the Pittsburgh Steelers football team, had unusual visual perception in an important match: "All of a sudden . . . I realized I was following the quarterback all the way—and the receiver, too. It just happened. It was like I had stepped into an entirely new dimension." Golfer Jack Fleck in his 1955 playoff victory over Ben Hogan reported, "As I looked at my putt, the hole looked as big as a wash tub. I suddenly became convinced I couldn't miss." And he didn't.

Such cases of extraordinary perception dramatize how many of our principles are involved in the "physical" act of perceiving. The athletes, for example, are strongly motivated to perform well and win, a motivation that invokes emotions and will. They have long training in the kinds of perception involved, and that training forms patterns at the vital, etheric level. Their minds are sharply focused on the task at hand. Intuitive perception may be activated by the intensity of concentration. The process of perception invokes powers at many levels, not only the physical.

In *The Future of the Body*, Michael Murphy, a leading figure in the human potential movement, describes paranormal capacities such as ESP, extraordinary movement abilities, unusual somatic awareness and self-regulation, and superabundant vitality. He believes that such powers are latent in us all and suggests attitudes and practices for developing them. Theosophy teaches that the whole human species is evolving, as are individual members of it. It has taken eons for each of our senses to develop. Although the focus is now on higher levels such as insight, intuition, and compassion, rather than on body, studies like those Murphy reports indicate that our physical abilities have unexpected potentials and can develop much farther than they have so far.

Mind over Matter

Attitudes, thoughts, feelings, and motivations that come from principles other than the physical have profound physical effects. Your child's face and the droop of her shoulders show you she is unhappy, and you know by the spring in your mother's walk that she is cheerful and glad to see you. Dancers deliberately dramatize the bodily effects of emotion, and conductors do so musically. If you have ever watched an animated conductor like Seiji Ozawa, you have seen the body almost dancing as it expresses the changing rhythms and moods of the music. Such movement as his springs from powerful feeling and subtle understanding of what is being played. As his body almost defies gravity, it does indeed appear to be a flying temple of the spirit.

A wealth of evidence indicates that thoughts, attitudes, motivations, and emotions affect physical health. It is well established that depression weakens the immune system and that positive, happy emotions improve it—laughter can even enhance healing. Visualization has been shown to decrease cancer cells. Meditation affects the blood volume and electrical activity in the frontal lobes of the brain and strengthens the immune system, among other physiological responses.

Belief is central to the effects of placebos. These are inert substances that patients think are medicine. Double-blind experiments, in which neither the person administering the dose nor the patient taking it knows what is being ingested, have shown that placebos can improve conditions such as postoperative pain, cough, angina pectoris, headache, seasickness, anxiety, mood changes, and the common cold (Murphy 247). Various kinds of pain can be relieved by placebos, as can the symptoms of depression and anxiety.

On the other hand, placebos can also bring on symptoms. They can both stimulate and relieve breathing difficulties in asthmatics. An asthma attack can result from a patient inhaling a simple saline solution that he or she thinks is allergenic, and inhaling a placebo can return them to their normal condition (Murphy 251).

The placebo effect shows that volitions, motivations, and mental images can affect the body. Experiments with placebos have convinced many psychologists and medical practitioners that we have untapped resources for restoring ourselves to health. Writer Norman Cousins said, "The placebo is an emissary between the will to live and the body but the emissary is expendable" (Murphy 249). In other words, the will to live can act on the body even without a placebo.

Physical Anomalies

Cases of religious stigmata dramatize the effect of higher orders of consciousness on the physical body. Wounds that correspond to

Christ's crucifixion wounds have been objectively studied by doctors, medical researchers, and churchmen since 1930, and many more were reported before then. These stigmata are bruises, welts, and bleeding wounds on the hands and sides, as well as puncture wounds on the head and back, representing Christ's crown of thorns, scourging, nailing to the cross, and piercing by a lance. Some people with stigmata bleed every Friday, some on particular Fridays, and some every day. One of the best-studied and most dramatic examples is Padre Pio (1887–1968), a member of the Capuchin order in Italy, whose fame spread around the world. For a time, blood oozed from his stigmata spasmodically, but from 1918 until his death, the phenomenon was permanent and frequently photographed. The Church of Rome, in a move to deemphasize the importance of such phenomena, restricted Padre Pio's priestly office for a time. But after more study of the stigmata, he was again allowed to function as a priest. Many objective professors and doctors who examined him attested to the genuineness of his condition. In his later years, hundreds or thousands of people gathered daily to be near him (Murphy 492–94).

Stigmata-like phenomena that are not religious sometimes occur in clinical situations. For example, a psychiatric patient showed indentations on his arms that looked like rope marks. These appeared whenever he relived an episode during which he was tied to a bed to inhibit sleepwalking (Murphy 235). Scars appeared on the back of another patient in the place where, years before, her father had scratched her with his fingernails. The scars appeared whenever she was expecting a visit from her father (234).

Even more dramatic examples of the power of inner states on the body come from studies of people with multiple-personality disorder. In this psychiatric condition, different ego states alternately control the body. As patients switch from one personality to another, their gestures, carriage, voice, mental set, emotions, and self-identity change dramatically. Often they take on the guise of the opposite sex or a child state. They sometimes show remarkable physical alterations. Some change from right-handedness to left-handedness. Allergies come and go. One patient was highly allergic to citrus fruit, but in one of her personalities she could eat and ingest an orange with no ill effect. Another woman itched and her eyes teared whenever she contacted cats. But in another ego state she could play with them, even be scratched and licked, with no symptoms (Murphy 242).

In some patients, visual acuity was much better in certain ego-states than in others, and some patients had different eyeglasses for different personalities. In some cases significant changes in the shape and curvature of the eyes were found in different ego states. One patient in her five-year-old personality, but not in the others, showed "lazy eye" syndrome that normally appears only in young children (Murphy 243).

Biomedical researcher Jeanne Achterberg related a story that was in the news some years ago. A woman was brutally attacked in the desert. One of her arms was cut off before she was left to die. Somehow she did not bleed to death but wandered for three days in the desert before she was found. When asked how she managed to survive such severe injuries, she said she didn't know. She just kept thinking of herself as the bionic woman—a somewhat robot-like "superwoman" in a television series. Achterberg used this seeming miracle as an instance of the power of imaging (Achterberg 1997). Such instances illustrate the immense power of inner states on the body. As writer Norman Cousins pointed out, "The human mind converts ideas and expectations into biochemical realities. . . . Beliefs affect biology" (Knaster 54).

Another provocative line of research was conducted by professor and researcher Ian Stevenson. (One of the most popular of his nine books on reincarnation is *Twenty Cases Suggestive of Reincarnation* [Charlottesville: University Press of Virginia, 1974].) He published descriptions of cases of children who claimed to remember previous lives and who had birthmarks relevant to these memories. Stevenson is known for his meticulous research matching past-life memories in children with their supposed earlier families and lives.

Stevenson studied birthmarks among children whose memories of an earlier life had been verified. In a significant number of cases, birthmarks that corresponded to the means of death of the earlier personality were found on the child. Stevenson reports in detail the case of Chanai Choomalaiwong, born in central Thailand in 1967. Beginning at age three, Chanai would take the role of a teacher when playing with children, and he claimed that he had been a teacher in his past life as Bua Kai. He lived in the town of Khao Phra, had parents, a wife, and children there, and was killed on his way to school.

Before he was four, Chanai was taken to a town near Khao Phra. He then led the way to the house where he claimed to have lived. The couple who lived in the house verified the information about Bua Kai and the way he died. Further research uncovered the fact that Bua Kai was indeed a school teacher, but he was also a gangster—a dangerous profession—and he had two guns. Also, he had affairs with women whose husbands probably objected. In any case, whatever the motive, he was shot in the head as he rode his bicycle to school one day.

A doctor and Bua Kai's wife and brother saw the body and agreed that the bullet had entered the back of the head and exited above the left eye. A small round birthmark on the back of Chanai's head corresponded to the bullet's point of entry on Bua Kai. There was a larger irregular birthmark on the front of Chanai's head where the bullet would have exited. These markings correspond to the fact that a wound of entry is almost always smaller than a wound of exit.

For well-authenticated cases such as this one, Stevenson posits several explanations, such as various forms of extrasensory perception. However, in his judgment actual reincarnation is the most plausible (Stevenson 38–41).

Consciousness and the Brain

Jonathan gives his wife Selma a bath and dresses her. He feeds her breakfast spoonful by spoonful as she stares at him blankly. Then he tries to put her in her coat, but she refuses to put her arms into the sleeves. He gets it on her and tries to lead her to the car. She pulls away and tries to scratch him. He finally almost carries her to the car and starts the short drive to her doctor's office. As he slows down for a stop sign, Selma opens the door and jumps out of the car. He pulls over and rushes to where she is lying. She has landed on a grassy slope and rolled part way down it, unhurt. She tries to claw him as he carries her back to the car.

Selma has Altzheimer's disease. Only three years ago she was working at a brilliant career in public relations. Jonathan realizes that his once intelligent, responsive, loving wife must now be put into a nursing home. Altzheimer's severely damages the brain, just as strokes, head injuries, alcohol, and drugs can. The damage can so profoundly affect the patient's personality that he or she seems to be a different person.

The brain, as has long been known, is intimately associated with consciousness. The close correlation between body, mind, and emotion has led scientific materialists to believe that thought and feelings are only the results of brain action. This view sees consciousness as a by-product of matter, an accidental effect of complex biochemical combinations. As explained in chapter 2, esoteric philosophy and Theosophy hold that consciousness is primary. It is everywhere, in everything, and all material forms are conscious in some degree. Some physicists agree. They theorize that consciousness is at the quantum level of matter. It is well known that quantum objects such as electrons appear sometimes as particles and sometimes as waves. These scientists hold that the wave aspect has rudimentary properties of mind, so that consciousness appears with matter even at this most fundamental level.

Theosophy and transpersonal psychology also differ from scientific materialism regarding the relationship between brain and mind. The brain is so closely connected with consciousness that changes in the brain obviously affect conscious experience. Scientific materialists infer from this connection that the brain produces consciousness, that it secretes thought as the liver secretes bile. But according to Theosophy and transpersonal psychology, consciousness or the mind uses the brain as its instrument. The psychiatrist Stanislov Grof compares the brain to a television set (Nelson 8). For an undistorted picture and clear sound, every component of the set must be functioning properly. A faulty set gives faulty reception. But television programs are not generated by the set; it is only an instrument that picks up the signals behind the programs. Similarly, the brain registers events in consciousness, but it does not generate thought.

Consciousness and Fields

As explained in chapters 1 and 2, Theosophy holds that the physical world is the densest of several levels of existence and is the only one the normal senses can perceive. Though sometimes called "planes," these levels can be thought of as fields in space, each with a characteristic type of matter.

All living things are surrounded by electrical fields. Electrical readings of trees show daily, monthly, and seasonal rhythms of electrical fluctuation. Such changes are sometimes predictable, making it possible to foresee the productivity of crops. Electrical fields around human subjects have also been studied, and alterations in them have been found to correspond with the subjects' mental and physical conditions. Kirlian photography shows a corona of electrical discharge around humans and all other living things.

Human consciousness can interact with electrical and other fields. One of the most interesting research projects demonstrating this fact was conducted by Elmer Green, formerly of the Menninger Clinic, who is known for his studies of biofeedback and consciousness (Green 67–71). He took a clue from a passage in the Theosophical classic *The Mahatma Letters* (217–18), where a method for training student monks is described. The student sits on a stool insulated from the earth in a darkened room. In front of him is a wall covered by a mirror of highly polished metal, mostly copper. A magnet is suspended over his head. He sits there and gazes at the wall to develop "lucidity."

From this account, Green got the idea that both electrical and magnetic fields might be used to study consciousness. He set up a laboratory with four mirrored walls, one in front, one in back, one above, and one below the subject. These were fitted with electrometers to measure changes in electrical potential. Subjects were also hooked to measuring devices. This "Copper Wall Project" took place over a twelve-year period.

Green chose two groups of meditators as subjects for his studies, half ordinary or "regular" people and half "exceptional" people, nationally known as sensitives or healers. He looked for electrical field disturbances on the walls or within the subjects. The regular subjects showed nothing unusual, but with several of the healers, unexplained voltage spikes occurred both in their bodies and from all four walls. Some spikes were as much as 100,000 times greater than ordinary voltage from the brain and 10,000 times greater than from the heart. Another interesting finding was that women felt energized when the magnet over their heads was placed with the south pole up and inhibited when the north pole was up, whereas men reacted in exactly the opposite way. This study suggests that male and female bodies respond differently to magnetic fields and, more importantly, that consciousness interacts with such fields.

Research like Green's opens the door to the possibility of other unknown fields interacting with consciousness. Such fields would help to explain ESP and other phenomena that do not fit into the materialistic paradigm. William Tiller, crystallographer at Stanford University, after studying the data on ESP, concluded that "we seem to be dealing with new energy fields completely different from those known to us via conventional science" (60). The neuropsychiatrist Shafica Karagulla also sees evidence for fields beyond the ones known to science. She says that "research points significantly to the fact that in addition to the electrical and magnetic fields which surround all physical events, there are other types of energies and frequencies that are as yet undetectable by any instrumentation so far developed" (Karagulla and Kunz 5). The "other types of energies" she refers to are the etheric, astral, and mental fields described in Theosophical literature.

Building on knowledge of the relationship between living things and electrical fields, Rupert Sheldrake has proposed a "morphogenetic field" of energies, so far undetected by science, which guides the development of embryos and the structure of living forms (Sheldrake 109–113). This field molds developing cells, tissues, and organisms. For example, in a chicken embryo, tissue around what will become the heart begins to beat before the heart is formed. This anticipation suggests a field that guides the developmental process forming a heart from cells that have not yet become specialized. The vital or etheric body, according to Blavatsky and later investigators, is just such a guiding matrix. It provides a mold or pattern along the lines of which the dense physical body develops. Blavatsky sometimes called the vital body the "model body."

The Etheric Double and Subtle Energy

The dense physical world is closely related to its subtler vital or etheric field, which is part of the physical. The vital or etheric body serves as a bridge between the physical and other levels. According to observers of superphysical energies like C. W. Leadbeater and Dora Kunz, physical impulses are transmitted to the vital, which in turn transmits them to the higher centers of matter and consciousness. Conversely, emotional, mental, and spiritual impulses also affect the brain through this level.

To clairvoyant vision, the vital body looks like a web of fine, bright lines of force. Their color is pale blue-gray or violet-gray, somewhat luminous, and shimmering like heat waves. The vital body penetrates the dense physical and extends two or three inches beyond it in the average person. This double is a rarefied counterpart of the physical body. Each organ of the physical body has an etheric duplicate. Currents of *prana* or "life energy" flow through these etheric organs, vitalizing their functions and energizing the dense body and its organs. Trained medical clairvoyants can sometimes diagnose an illness that appears at the etheric level but only later shows up in dense physical symptoms.

Knowledge of subtle energy, as it is now sometimes called, has a long history. In China, it is called *chi* (spelled *qi* in the newer Pinyan transcription of Chinese, corresponding with *ki* in Japanese) and is associated with parts of the body, breath, acupuncture, and martial arts such as tai chi. It is the force behind extraordinary lifting, breaking, and leaping in these arts. In Polynesia, *mana* denotes "a spiritual power in all things" to varying degrees. The ancient Egyptians acknowledged a mysterious fluid called *sa,* which could be transmitted by the laying-on of hands. It is called *prana* in India, where Yoga postures and breathing exercises were designed to affect its flow. Peoples around the world have recognized a force that is not within conventional Western knowledge today.

Some Westerners, however, have recognized the existence of a subtle energy and called it by various names. Anton Mesmer in the eighteenth century called it "animal magnetism" and directed it for healing. Baron von Reichenbach in the early nineteenth century conducted experiments on *od* or "odic force," which many of his subjects could see as light or colors emanating from people and things. Wilhelm Reich in the first part of the twentieth century researched "orgone energy" for its energizing and healing properties. He invented an "orgone blanket" made from alternate layers of wool and steel-wool padding. Patients who used it thought that this blanket created a field for healing and well-being.

Contemporary versions of Reich's device have been created by the psychologist Serge King, who reports that an energy field is created whenever metallic and nonmetallic layers are joined together (84). One of his devices is a "space blanket," which consists of layers of aluminum foil between layers of plastic wrap. Patients report being energized and receiving healing effects from lying under it. Another such device with reported healing effects is a "manabloc," a sheet of metal immersed in resin. Once King accidentally cut his finger with a carving knife. The cut was so deep that blood spurted out for several feet. He made a pressure bandage from a napkin and then immediately placed the finger over a manabloc. Within minutes the pain subsided. Within an hour the napkin could be removed. Ordinarily he would have needed several stitches for such a wound, but after an hour the edges had already begun to seal together. By the next day the cut looked like a surface scratch (74).

Therapeutic Touch

Therapeutic Touch (TT) is a technique supplementary to conventional forms of medicine, in which practitioners typically move their hands a few inches from the patient's body to manipulate the flow of etheric energy through the vital body. Practitioners report that, while treating patients, they feel warm, cool, or tingling sensations in their hands, which they interpret as indicating the flow of energy. They become sensitive to slight variations and changes in the patient's field and learn to work with subtle energies to improve its condition. In giving a treatment, they draw, not on their own energy, but on prana, the universal energy pervading all living things. Dolores Krieger, Professor Emerita at New York University and a founder of the TT movement, explains that "the healer sensitively draws upon the universal energies that are the backdrop of all living events and within which both healer and healee [patient] are figures sharing a unitary nature" (45). A number of research projects and academic dissertations and theses have shown that the technique can indeed be effective in promoting health.

In one study of TT, two groups of volunteer subjects were slightly wounded on the arm. In a lab, they were asked to put their arms through a hole in a wall each day for a short period. For one group, in the room on the other side of the wall, out of sight of the subjects, a TT healer treated the wounds by moving her hands above the skin with the intention to heal. The other group, who were controls, received no treatment while their arms were through the hole. This method ruled out the effect of suggestion. As expected by TT practitioners, the treated subjects healed significantly faster than the controls.

Dolores Krieger relates a time when she treated a wheelchair-bound patient whose spinal cord was severed, so that he had no neural circuits in his legs and could feel nothing in them. He did not know her and was unfamiliar with TT. Yet, though he could not see what she was doing, he described feeling heat in just the areas where Krieger was treating him, and where she, herself, also felt heat. Kirlian photography shows flares from the hands of the healer giving a TT treatment, confirming that something objective is taking place.

You can sense the prana in your own body. When you feel energized or "alive," prana is coursing vigorously through your vital body. When you feel exhausted or "drained," the currents are weak and sluggish. Diaphragmatic breathing (from the belly) brings in prana and can make you feel more energetic. It can also calm you and smooth the flow from the etheric to higher centers.

You can also sensitize yourself to the energy flow in your hands by a simple exercise (Krieger 24). Sit or stand comfortably with the palms of your hands facing each other. Bring your palms close together so that only about one-quarter of an inch separates them. Now bring them about four inches apart. Then with slow, continuous motion, again bring both hands close together. Once again separate your hands by about six inches, and again move them close together. Finally, separate your hands by about eight inches and bring them together with slight bouncy movements, so that they move toward each other one or two inches at a time. Notice any sensations in your hands. Do the entire exercise several times. Most people get a strong sense of a field between their hands.

Another exercise is done with a partner (Krieger, *The Therapeutic Touch* 59). One of you is a sender and the other a receiver. You sit facing one another. The receiver places the back of her hands on her knees while the sender places his hand a few inches above her hands, palms down. The sender imagines energy just over his right shoulder and brings it down to his elbow, then his wrist, then his hand. He focuses the energy in the center of his palm. The receiver "listens" for any change she feels in her palms. Then the partners switch roles. Many people get a definite sensation of receiving or sending energy from this activity.

Chakras

Emotional, mental, and intuitional impressions register in your consciousness, just as do physical sensations. Centers of consciousness called "charkas" integrate and transmit impressions between the dense physical, etheric, astral, and mental levels. Chakras are centers in our subtle bodies that have been recognized for millennia by Yoga philosophy, Indian and Tibetan tantrism, and Chinese esotericism. They appear to clairvoyants as spinning wheels or vortices of energy at superphysical levels, like whirlpools in the aura. They are flower-like, with "petals" of different streams of energy, and are described as lotuses in Indian literature. The best general description of them is that by C. W. Leadbeater in his book *The Chakras*.

FIGURE I

Each chakra is located at a specific area of the body (figure 1), is associated with a physical organ, and interacts with an endocrine gland. You have probably felt your solar plexus chakra, a center that is easily disturbed by emotion. When you feel you have been hit "in the pit of your stomach," or an emptiness in that area when you are exhausted, you are feeling a condition of this chakra. Or you may have felt sensations from your heart chakra. Recall a quiet, relaxed situation, perhaps on a walk or sitting before a fire, when you shared thoughts and feelings with someone you love. As you dwell on this memory for a while, you may notice a warm, radiant, expanding sensation in the middle of your chest, where this chakra is situated. The heart chakra is associated with affection and devotion.

The chakras act as funnels to draw in prana or life force, and different kinds of forces pour through each of them (Leadbeater 47–49). By interfacing between the dense and subtle realms, they synchronize the physical body and consciousness with etheric, emotional, and mental realms. All are connected by superphysical energies flowing through the spinal cord. They are associated with different states of consciousness, and are involved in registering spiritual experiences and other higher impressions on the brain. Spiritual development is accompanied by intensification of the activity of the chakras and the forces they channel, as Eastern religious traditions have long recognized.

Hiroshi Motoyama is a Japanese researcher who studies chakras and superphysical energy, which he calls "psi energy." He invented an instrument to detect chakra energy generated in the body or transmitted from it. This instrument registers minute energy changes of electrical, magnetic, and optical nature that occur near the subject. In one experiment, Motoyama placed the electrodes of the instrument close to the front of a meditator's chest, over the area where the heart chakra is located (276–78). When the subject was in a relaxed state, a positive electrical potential was generated. Then she was asked to concentrate on the heart chakra and to press a button when she had the sensation of energy being emitted from that chakra, which she felt regularly in her meditations. Pressing the button caused a mark to be made on the chart that showed her measurements. At the spot where this mark appeared on the chart, a photoelectric cell showed a weak light being generated in the light-proof room, and energy of high potential and frequency was registered as coming from her.

Such data imply that, associated with the charkas, is indeed a superphysical or psi energy that can generate measurable light and electricity. Motoyama predicts that subsequent studies into the nature of psi energies "will lead to considerable change in our views of matter and body, of human beings, and of the world itself" (279).

The Body and the Self

The body is not an inert, unresponsive material object—a fact suggested by the story of Pinocchio. In the original version of that tale, Pinocchio was lazy, like his inert wooden body. He did not want to go to school or exert himself. His friend Jiminy Cricket warned him that he would end up in either a hospital or a jail if he did not go to school and better himself. Pinocchio, however, did not want to hear this, so he killed poor Jiminy (who later came back to life). It seems that even a wooden boy needs to be animated by more than his body.

Our body is not a wooden doll. Like Pinocchio, we cannot live just at the physical level. The body works within the whole self and is intimately connected with other powers of the self. We never have a physical experience without some emotion and some mental interpretation of it. In us, the etheric, astral, and mental are integrated with our consciousness at the physical level. Each of us is a system of interdependent force fields that respond to changes in consciousness. Shafika Karagulla used the metaphor of a living tapestry for the complex of interacting processes at work within us all the time: "The interweaving of the three fields of the personal self, together with their vehicle, the physical body, gives us a picture of human life which can be compared to a moving, four-dimensional tapestry, whose warp and woof are composed of threads of differing qualities and textures, and whose patterns shift and change as they cut across the path of time" (Karagulla and Kunz 27).

We sometimes unconsciously think of the body as ourselves. Its needs, wants, and comfort are the focus and the motivation of much that we do. But Karagulla agrees with Theosophy that the body is an instrument for the use of the whole self. It has been compared to a horse on which we ride. It must be well fed and cared for, but the rider, the self, must direct it. The body is indeed a temple of the spirit, a traveling temple, as Ram Dass called it. It is part of our whole self and cannot exist alone any more than could the heart or liver.

The place of the body in the whole self is evident in an experience called "flow." Imagine that you are a rock climber. You have been trained and know how to use your body and your equipment to ascend to higher rocks or to catch yourself if you should slip. You have climbed above the easy stretch on the lower part of the mountain. Now you must use all your skills to boost yourself from rock to rock up a precipitous cliff. You are fully concentrated on what you are doing. You are highly aware of the boulders and dangerous rolling pebbles you encounter as well as of your own body. But you are not self-conscious, not thinking of yourself or of what a good climber you are or that you could get hurt. You are completely absorbed in climbing. Yet you know instinctively where to place your pick and where your feet should go, and your movements are spontaneous and unpremeditated. Even though the situation is dangerous, you are joyous and free. You are in a state of flow.

When they are in the flow, people are happy, although they do not think about it until afterwards. The University of Chicago professor Mihaly Csikszentmihalyi describes flow as an optimal experience that gives deep enjoyment (9). He points out that this enjoyment comes from achieving mastery over oneself, and it spills over into one's general happiness in life. He says, "Whether we are happy depends on inner harmony, not on the controls we are able to exert over the great forces of the universe."

Flow can come while people are making music, dancing, creating art, playing chess or tennis, sailing, or even performing routine movements on an assembly line. Csikszentmihalyi studied flow in such diverse groups as runners and athletes, surgeons, engineers, champion chess players, and even file clerks. He found reports of flow in ethnic groups as diverse as Korean women, Japanese teenagers, and Navaho shepherds. According to his research, just the right proportion of skill and challenge is needed; the activity must not be too easy or too hard. Motivation for doing the activity comes from the sheer pleasure of it, not from money, recognition, or any product it engenders. Performing with flow is its own reward.

Being completely absorbed in the activity with no thought of oneself does not mean loss of consciousness or loss of self, but rather a loss of consciousness *of* self. Somehow you do just the right thing without thinking about it or feeling that you are doing anything at all. It just happens. As a rock climber put it, "You are so involved in what you are doing [that] you aren't thinking of yourself as separate from the immediate activity" (Csikszentmihalyi 53). But though it seems effortless, acting in flow requires considerable physical exertion and disciplined mental activity. The body, emotions, and mind are perfectly coordinated and animated by a single urge.

Csikszentmihalyi describes this as "the way people describe their state of mind when consciousness is harmoniously ordered" (6). The word "flow," in addition to describing this subjective state, is apt for describing how the movement of different energies within the body and personality flow together in a highly focused state. It also applies to the merging of action and awareness that characterizes this state.

The term "zone" is used by sports people to denote a similar altered state or peak performance that is smooth and spontaneous and accompanied by exhilaration. Extraordinary abilities sometimes occur when an athlete is in the zone. In this state, people feel that time slows down and events are intuited in advance. They feel that there is "a space beyond ordinary space" intimately connected with both mind and body.

When you are in the zone or in flow, your body and mind work together in an integrated fashion. Sometimes powers from a source beyond mind and ego are accessed, showing that our personal selves are part of a greater whole Self. Quarterback John Brodie describes times when the entire team "leaps up a few levels" and there is "a tremendous rush of energy across the field." The energy of all eleven players flows in the same direction and creates a "special concentration of power" that is felt by everyone, even the people in the stands (Murphy 106).

Body and Spirit

Buddhism teaches that enlightenment is possible only in a physical body. Buddhists are therefore grateful for being in human form. For them, it is a rare privilege to have heard the Buddha's teaching and to have the opportunity to devote themselves to living in the physical world according to that teaching. Theosophy and Yoga philosophy agree that the physical as well as the other principles—our whole psychophysical complex—is involved in the spiritual life. We need to exert effort at all levels to achieve harmony with the Self.

The body is not only a necessary and vital part of the whole self, it is also an instrument of the spirit. As mentioned, Blavatsky pointed out that atma in itself cannot be active in the world; it needs vehicles of matter to express itself. The body is especially important, for Blavatsky says that it is the vehicle for all the other principles. We are complete only with a physical body, which provides a focus for all the higher principles. Through the body, atma expresses powers that are only potential at higher levels. All these powers will be actualized more and more as we, both as individuals and as a species, continue to evolve. Taimni emphasizes the importance of life in a physical body for spiritual evolution: "The life lived on the physical plane is thus the most significant . . . and this is no doubt due to the fact that it reflects and specially embodies the life of the Atma, the highest aspect of the individuality" (171).

The way we live and the inner states we develop can make the body an instrument of the spirit and bring it into harmony with the higher principles. The body affects all the principles, just as they affect the body. The Theosophist Clara Codd pointed out this mutual influence when she said that the body "is a living, sensitive thing, though not truly ourselves; and whilst in living communication with the soul, reflects and affects, as far as possible, the powers and conditions of its partner" (221).

The body has, however, a life of its own that does not always synchronize with our higher inclinations. The body may want to eat or sleep too much or to avoid anything strenuous or challenging. It needs to be trained by gentle discipline. People sometimes resist discipline, especially in these times when personal freedom is so highly valued. But every spiritual tradition insists on some kind of discipline. The spiritual life offers freedom *through* the body, not *of* the body. As the body is tamed to respond to what we as the self choose, we become free from its demands and can use it more effectively.

The first step in taking control of the body is to realize that it is a living vehicle with tendencies and habits of its own, which we must respect. Then we need to realize, not just think but really know, that we are not primarily the body but that it is only part of ourselves. By disidentifying from it we can better have dominion over it. Through gentle but steady pressure, we can refine its appetites and change its habits.

A clean life sensitizes the body and the other lower vehicles to influences from subtler and more spiritual aspects of the self. Many people who choose a spiritual way of life become vegetarians, refrain from tobacco, alcohol, and nonmedicinal drugs, and are chaste, though not necessarily celibate, in their sex lives. Many religious traditions ordain such practices as minimum conditions for aspirants. Such a way of life interacts with the practice of meditation. Taimni explains that "intense concentration of the mind, combined with an ardent aspiration of the soul, polarizes all the energies working in the lower vehicles in the direction of the higher self, and thus makes the influx of the subtler forces into the physical brain possible" (58).

Over time, the process of meditation awakens and enhances the chakras. It leads to the merging of the personality with the transpersonal self and with atma. Such awakening and merging shows in the physical appearance of great souls. Anagarika Govinda relates that the Buddha's body "is said to have been of such unearthly beauty and radiance, that even the golden robes which were offered to him lost their luster" (*Foundations of Tibetan Buddhism* 69). For the enlightened one, the body became, as it eventually will for all of us, not just a shadow from the light of atma, but its luminous reflection.

The Emotions: The Powerhouse of Life

Those who enter the gates of heaven are not beings who have no passions or who have curbed their passions, but those who have cultivated an understanding of them.

William Blake

Jimmy is crying hard and asking for a bandage. He has just lost a tooth for the first time and is scared. A little blood on his lip mixes with the tears. Miss Martin puts her arm around him and tells him that it is all right, that another tooth is growing in. But Jimmy keeps sobbing and asking for a bandage. Miss Martin phones Jimmy's mother, who speaks with him and tries to comfort him, but to no avail. Finally Miss Martin goes to the first-aid cabinet and gets a Band-Aid, which she sticks on Jimmy's upper lip. He stops crying and looks at her. She again tells him that losing a tooth is normal and another is growing in. He listens. She leads him to the reading table and together they read *The Little Train That Could*, his favorite story. Soon he is playing a version of "Go Fish" that teaches reading skills, along with other children at the special-education learning center.

Maggie Martin, who works with small groups of special-education children, is warm and sympathetic and aware of her students' moods and problems. In choosing an activity for these emotionally volatile kids, she first thinks of how they will react. She finds ways to get them excited about what they are going to do. She is generally cheerful and outgoing, but sometimes the children are exasperating and she gets irritated and angry. She expresses her feelings appropriately by patiently letting them know what they have done wrong, not in outbursts followed by regret. She is tactful and thinks of the children's point of view when she has to correct them. She is committed to helping these children and takes her vocation very seriously. But she can also be spontaneous and playful. She often sings and dances with the children and plays silly word games with them. There is a lot of laughter in her classroom.

Maggie's relations with friends and family have many of the same qualities she shows while teaching. She is empathetic and understanding but also loves fun and leisure activities such as funny movies and rock music. She seldom thinks out her position on any issue that comes up but discovers what her position is as she expresses her feelings. She is apt to reject ideas that conflict with her feelings and can sometimes be blind to facts. Though she is warm and has many friends, she needs their approval and is sensitive to criticism, praise, or indifference.

Maggie would be classified as emotional and extravert on the Myers-Briggs Personality Inventory. Her first consideration is the effect of what she does on other people. Emotion is often linked with the word "social," implying that emotional responses are most often evoked in relationships. But Maggie also gives high priority to her personal values. She feels emotions intensely and lives more by how she feels than by what she thinks. Women tend to be more emotional than men, but both men and women with emotional orientation like Maggie's are found in many walks of life, especially as clergy, sales persons, actors, and homemakers.

The Color of Emotions

All forms of life have some degree of feeling or sentience, but we humans experience it in more varied ways than other organisms—even primates, who have a rich emotional life. We can feel the ecstatic joy of falling in love and also the profound suffering of losing a loved one. We can feel terror because of an intruder in the night and the deep peace of prayerfully reaching out to the divine. We are sensitive emotional beings with endless shadings of feelings.

All our experience is colored by our emotions, which set the tone of our daily experience. An old Japanese tale tells of a samurai who challenged a Zen master to explain heaven and hell. The master called him a lout and said he could not waste time on such a person as he. The samurai flew into a rage, pulled his sword, and threatened to kill the monk. "That," the monk said calmly, "is hell." Seeing the point, the samurai sheathed his sword, bowed, and thanked the monk for leading him to this insight. "And that," said the monk, "is heaven." Our emotional reactions do make our hell and heaven.

People everywhere react emotionally in the same way to traumas like war. Disorders like posttraumatic stress syndrome are not limited to any particular culture. Children, whether in Northern Ireland or Israel, may seem cheerful and happy at play. But they have nightmares and relive the violence they have experienced, as do veterans from wars like that in Vietnam. We all exhibit the same kinds of emotions.

Darwin recognized the universality of emotion long before the present-day concerns with its negative psychological effects. People from cultures around the world can recognize certain facial expressions as indicative of particular emotions, and that is true even of people from preliterate societies, who could not have learned to associate the expressions with emotions from television or movies. If people are shown pictures of faces expressing the basic emotion of fear, anger, sadness, or enjoyment, they can identify the emotion being expressed. The range of human emotions is very wide, including warmth, tenderness, anger, hostility, hope, disappointment, success, failure, joy, sadness, loneliness, lightheartedness, depression, regret, remorse, and resentment. Life would be flat and colorless without the emotions, strong or subtle, that tinge all our experience.

Emotions tend to come and go quickly, whereas moods last longer. Moods are more muted and can be a background for whatever we are doing or thinking. Temperament is a yet longer-term propensity to evoke a given emotion or mood. Moods tend to replace one another in our awareness, but we all have a background murmur of feelings that mark our basic temperament: optimism or pessimism, cheerfulness or gloominess, affection or dislike, fearfulness or boldness. For example, a curmudgeon is an ill-tempered old man, and a "Pollyanna" is one who is unceasingly optimistic. Mothers know that some babies are placid or testy from birth or, even before birth, in the womb. Some are timid, others bold, some happy, others melancholy. Actress Goldie Hawn claimed that she was "born with a tickle of joy." Studies show that babies' temperaments are more important for how quickly they calm down when they are crying than anything their mothers do to soothe them. Though emotions come and go, this background of emotionality remains to define our temperament or disposition.

What Is Emotion?

Psychologists have quibbled for more than a century on the precise meaning of the word "emotion." Like consciousness, emotion is unmistakable in our experience but hard to define. The word comes from the Latin *movēre,* "to move," and *ex,* "away"; hence, "to move away." Emotion has been called the affective (influencing) aspect of consciousness, as opposed to the cognitive (knowing) or the conative (willing). Some physiological psychologists define it in terms of the physical changes that accompany different emotional states. The *Oxford English Dictionary* defines emotion as "any agitation or disturbance of mind, feeling, passion; any vehement or excited state." However, this definition does not cover the quieter, subtler emotions that are a constant background hum in our stream of consciousness.

The psychologist Daniel Goleman takes the word *emotion* to refer to "a feeling and its distinctive thoughts, psychological and biological states, and range of propensities to act" (289). His definition shows how closely emotion is linked with thought and action. As indicated in chapter 2, the interconnections among these three are constant. You yourself probably know that emotional distress or chronic "toxic emotions" can cause illness. People in psychotherapy working intensively with emotional problems often develop physical symptoms as well. Usually our thoughtful, reflective side works harmoniously with the emotions, though we are sometimes aware of a conflict between mind and emotion, head and heart. But you may not realize that an emotional component—whether of boredom, enthusiasm, anxiety, or satisfaction—is present in all your thought, even that devoted to something quite abstract like mathematics.

We almost never experience pure emotion uncolored by thought, just as we do not experience sensation uninterpreted by the mind. When a loud thump wakes you up in the night, you may feel the emotion of surprise or fright before your mind starts figuring out what it was. If you get a shock, such as hearing of the sudden death of a close friend, you may have a moment of pure grief and shock before you start thinking about it. But usually we experience emotion, bodily changes, and thought all intertwined. As explained in chapter 2, our etheric, astral, and mental fields interpenetrate and interact with one another. The interactions among these three are almost instantaneous. Although each has its distinctive characteristics, they are not isolated from one another. Any disturbance ripples through them all.

Emotion as Energy

According to Freud and other psychotherapists, emotions and desire represent psychic energy. Freud called it "libido" and thought of it as basically sexual in nature. Clairvoyant investigation confirms the Theosophical teaching that emotions are truly energies that we transmit through the emotional field. Dora Kunz says, "To me vitality, feeling, and thinking are forms of energy." She believes that clairvoyance brings otherwise invisible wavelengths and frequencies within the range of perception. Although emotional energy, like prana, has never been captured by the instruments of physical science, it is real energy.

Whenever you feel an emotion, such as anger, a vibration of a particular frequency is set up in your aura and produces a characteristic color. This process has been compared to fireworks because different chemicals added to gunpowder give off different colors when ignited. For example, barium glows with green light and strontium gives off scarlet. Similarly, the aura lights up with various colors in response to various emotions. Emotions also stir up characteristic densities of the subtle matter associated with the field. Inspiring emotions such as spiritual aspiration evoke a subtler part within the field, whereas desires for material things stir up a denser part.

As explained in chapter 2, our emotional field or aura is our localization in a universal psychic field that is part of the structure of the universe, parallel to the electromagnetic, gravitational, and mental fields. When we feel an emotion, it affects our aura and also sends ripples out into this field. If the feeling is directed to a particular person, his or her aura may resonate to it, even at a distance. You think lovingly of Aunt Sally on the other side of the continent. Your aura turns mostly rose pink for the moment. Aunt Sally's aura receives the rose pink impulse and she feels affection. She may even think of you and phone you in response. Thus we are continually moving in our own emotional atmosphere and bombarding each other with our thoughts and feelings.

The atmosphere around us is filled with astral vibrations and energies caused by the emotions being projected by all the people in our environment and all over the world. When you send love to Aunt Sally, you not only affect Aunt Sally; you pour love into the entire field, which amplifies any similar energy that was already there. You have probably been aware of the contagious emotional excitement at a football game or a rock concert. You may also have felt the sense of peace and aspiration at a religious service or in an ancient cathedral. Such situations and places are charged with a particular kind of emotional energy.

On a larger scale, the atmosphere of a city or country, or even the whole world, can be charged so that millions are affected by it. Think of the fear generated by a stock-market crash or a threat of war. Think of the deaths of the Kennedys—Jack, Robert, and the young John—which millions of people watched or saw reported on television. Or think of the reaction to the real-time reports of the catastrophes in New York, Washington, and Pennsylvania on September 11, 2001. So many people flooding the emotional field with their distress no doubt affected the atmosphere of the entire earth, intensifying the emotions of everyone who watched with horror as the events unfolded. Powerful emotions from the emotional environment and from other individuals affect us all the time. We in turn contribute to the condition of the field and also to individuals toward whom we, consciously or unconsciously, project strong feelings.

Dora Kunz recommended a meditation to clear out unwanted feelings and contribute something positive to the emotional atmosphere. Two or three times a day, take a deep breath, quiet down, and center yourself. This takes only a moment in the midst of a busy life. Then think of yourself as a center of peace and radiate peaceful thoughts and feelings. By doing so, you not only release peace into the astral atmosphere, you also change your own emotional state to one of peace and happiness. An emotion such as love or peace flowing from the heart helps to clear out your own emotional disturbances. The resulting peaceful state invites higher consciousness and a link with the transpersonal Self.

Emotional Health and Awareness

Rather than speaking of virtue and vice, modern psychotherapists talk in terms of mental health. Good and evil certainly exist, and actions can be right or wrong. Yet viewing all things as either virtuous or vicious leads unrealistically to either self-righteousness or self-humiliation. On the other hand, we can view our own actions—and those of others—not just as meriting praise or blame, but as symptoms of underlying character traits that can be changed. This view may be more realistic and effective in promoting a sense of well-being free from both conceit and the pain of inappropriate fear, guilt, anger, or other overwhelmingly negative emotions.

The aura of an emotionally healthy person is balanced with harmonious thought and emotion and with a smooth flow of energy. According to transpersonal psychologist Frances Vaughan, prescriptions for maintaining emotional health are less well known than prescriptions for physical health, but they are no secret. We might divert the energy flow, sublimate it, or change its form to something helpful. But the first step is to become aware of our feelings, to identify them, and to be willing to experience them (*Inward Arc* 9–23).

Daniel Goleman has a different way of looking at emotional health. In his book *Emotional Intelligence*, he describes the characteristics of people who manage their emotional life intelligently. They have self-control and impulse control and can delay gratification, yet they have a zest for life and can motivate themselves. They are empathetic and can read others' feelings, and they handle relations with others well. They have ups and downs but are basically hopeful and optimistic. According to Goleman, it is not the avoidance of unpleasant feelings but the favorable ratio of positive to negative emotions that determines a sense of well-being. Joseph Campbell perhaps recognized and accepted this when he confided that he joyfully participated in the sorrows of life.

As noted above, emotion and desire represent psychic energy with a life of its own. Controlling this energy is hard, so managing and understanding emotions is a great concern in all schools of psychology and all spiritual disciplines. To influence emotional life is difficult because, as Freud discovered, much of our emotional life does not cross the threshold of awareness. Emotions seem to happen beyond our control; physiological reactions may appear even before one is conscious of the emotional reaction that provoked them. Yet, according to Vaughan, the basic principle for emotional health is to acknowledge your feelings because it is risky to ignore them (*Inward Arc* 12). You may have had a day when you were irritable and snapped at everyone without realizing what you were doing. If you become aware of what is happening, you are able to work with the feeling and not take it out on those around you. You can do something to change the background hum of your mood only when you know it is there.

However, sometimes emotion is so deeply buried that it is inaccessible to awareness. But as we become more aware of our inner life, previously unconscious emotions rise into consciousness, and we can sometimes catch the way emotions develop. Your irritability, for instance, may have come from news that your sister is seriously ill. You push the thought aside and do not attend to your anxiety and sadness. Yet they are just under the surface, destroying your peace of mind and erupting as unprovoked irritation. It is far better to attend to the basic feelings rather than to cover them over. Seeing their roots eliminates the misplaced negative emotion and lets you face the real problem. Awareness of emotions gives us more control over them and more freedom to create the state we desire.

When you observe that you are feeling a negative emotion like jealousy or anger, it is hard not to judge yourself harshly. But it is more helpful to identify the emotion—fear, anxiety, anger, discouragement, sadness—and examine it impersonally and watch how it arises. At first such observation takes practice and constant effort. But it is possible to cultivate an attitude of mindfulness, in which we stay in touch with what goes on within us while at the same time focusing on whatever we are doing at the moment. Taimni says that "gradually a consciousness develops in the background of our minds which seems to be aware of all the movements taking place in our emotional natures which like a silent spectator notes each movement, though it may not yet be able to control it" (73). Just watching impersonally without judging will sometimes take the energy away from a negative feeling. You simply let go of the feeling rather than keep it stirred up. Taimni says that if you thoroughly understand an emotion, you can cut off its motive power so that it dies.

We do not usually need to work with happy, positive emotions like affection, excited anticipation, or inspiration. But being more aware of what we are actually feeling is important in cultivating self-knowledge and mental health.

Repression

Denying or repressing feelings does not make them go away. Even consciously holding back feelings is not the best way to handle them because, when we try to suppress negative feelings, we inadvertently suppress all feelings; we shut out joy and affection as well. We do not need to linger on anger, irritation, and depression, nor to let them go unchecked, but simply to experience all emotions, without dwelling or acting on all of them.

In one study, some "unflappable" students were chosen as subjects because they were always upbeat and cheerful and didn't express negative feelings (Goleman 75–77). In part of the study, they had to complete an emotionally loaded sentence that began, "He kicked his roommate in the stomach. . . ." In another part, they listened to a list of words read aloud; many words on the list were emotionally neutral, but a few suggested hostility or sexual feelings. Physiological measurements taken during these tests showed that these "unflappables" had the usual signs of emotional upset, such as increased heart rate and blood pressure and sweating, when completing the sentence and hearing the emotionally charged words. They tuned out their emotions from awareness, yet their bodies responded emotionally. According to some schools of psychology, repressed desires and emotions of which you are not aware are forced into the subconscious, where they influence your thinking, behavior, and health in ways you do not suspect.

Emotion and Thought

Because of the strong connection between emotions and thoughts, emotion can disrupt the thinking process and overwhelm concentration.

You may have discovered from experience that too much anxiety leads to poor performance on academic tests. Among people in training to be air-traffic controllers, those with a high level of anxiety are the most apt to fail the training. On the other hand, positive emotions can improve mental performance. In one study, before subjects tried to solve a puzzle that predicts creative thinking, they were shown an amusing video that made them laugh. Seeing the video improved their performance and made them more creative.

Emotions guide thinking and shape decisions more than we realize. We tend to go with the decision that makes us feel good or that our "gut feeling" indicates. When you buy a new car or a house, or even a new sweater, probably you don't always choose the most practical and serviceable and the most economical, though your rational mind might tell you to. Within limits, you choose the one you like, the one that makes you feel good.

Ordinarily, the emotional faculty works with the rational mind to guide day-to-day decisions, and emotions help to guide us toward decisions that are right for us. A neurologist studied patients with an injury that impaired circuits between an important brain center for emotion (the amygdala) and the prefrontal lobes. For these patients, neural messages bypassed the part of the brain that ordinarily feeds emotion into a reaction. Although their IQ scores were not lowered by their injury, they made disastrous decisions in their personal lives and in business. Their likes and dislikes were blocked, and their emotional memory wiped out. They lived in a world of gray neutrality. And their lack of emotional reactions impaired their ability to make good decisions.

Roberto Assagioli found that some people benefit from thinking about their emotions and analyzing them. Such introspection leads them to consider the harm of uncontrolled expression and the regret that follows it. When you perceive an angry thought, he suggests that you ask yourself, "Will expressing this thought be useful? Will it help me achieve the outcome I want?" It is usually better to wait until the anger dies down before bringing up the issue to the person you are angry with. Compromises and solutions often emerge in a calm atmosphere.

Impulse Control

The unseen effects of emotions make it clear that we as individuals and the world as a whole would be better off if we all learned to curb our impulses. Daniel Goleman relates the pathetic story of Matilda, a fourteen-year-old who played a practical joke on her father (4). Her parents thought she was spending the night at a friend's house. When they came home at 1:00 AM, they heard noises from Matilda's room. Her father was unaware that she had decided not to stay away overnight, as he expected, but was hiding in her closet to surprise him. He reached for his pistol and went to investigate. When he came into the room, she jumped out with a loud noise. Acting on automatic impulse, he fired the pistol. The bullet entered her neck, and she died twelve hours later.

Such instantaneous reaction to hair-trigger shock, rage, or fear is probably a holdover from our distant ancestors who lived in the wild, where they needed to act instantaneously. It is seldom appropriate now. A particular neural pathway in the brain is involved with such automatic instant responses. Sometimes an impulse travels directly through the amygdala emotional center above the brain stem and reaches the prefrontal lobes only later. When it does so, the rational mind takes a moment or two longer than the emotions to register the triggering event, and we may react without thinking. To avoid automatic impulses that can lead to unhappy or even horrendous consequences, we need to be aware of our emotions and evaluate them.

Jack Kornfield, a psychotherapist and meditation teacher, recommends the Buddhist practice of "naming the demons" rather than acting on impulses and negative emotions (*Path with Heart* 84). In Buddhism, Mara, the god of darkness, represents all negative feelings and hindrances to clarity. The Christian Desert Fathers called such difficult emotions "demons." One of their masters said, "Stay watchful of gluttony and desire. And the demons of irritation and fear as well. The noonday demon of laziness and sleep will come after lunch each day, and the demon of pride will sneak up only when you have vanquished the other demons."

In the Buddhist practice, you recognize any habitual negative states, such as irritation or anxiety, as they arise and name them. When you experience greed, you say "greed," or you might name it "Hungry Ghost." This helps you to recognize and acknowledge each state and to notice what brings it about. Kornfield suggests watching for a particular demon, such as anger, for a week. You will find that, in time, rather than responding unthinkingly with anger, you will watch it arise for a moment and then decide how to respond. You insert a moment's reflection between the impulse and your action.

Impulse control affects many areas of life other than emotion in a crisis. To test their ability to delay gratification, the psychologist Walter Mischel gave four-year-olds a choice (Goleman 80–83). If they waited until he got back from an errand, they could have two marshmallows. If they did not wait for him, then they could have only the single marshmallow that was before them. Some of the children grabbed the one marshmallow as soon as the experimenter left the room. But some were able to wait for the seemingly endless fifteen or twenty minutes until he returned. They covered their eyes or rested their heads on their arms so that they could not see the temptation. Some talked to themselves, sang, or played games with their hands and feet. Some even tried to sleep.

A follow-up study was done with the same children years later, when they were adolescents. The emotional and social difference between the impulsive ones and those who waited was dramatic. Those who resisted temptation were now more socially competent, more self-assertive, better able to cope with frustration. They were more self-reliant, confident, and dependable. They were more likely to remain calm under stress. They liked challenges and stuck to projects in the face of difficulties. They were still able to delay gratification in pursuit of their goals. Impulse control and emotional intelligence are important for our ability to use our other mental faculties.

We all delay gratification from time to time when we focus on long-range goals. We put up with hunger pangs while we travel to our favorite restaurant for a late dinner. We give up sleep because of the baby's late feeding. We deny ourselves expensive pleasures to save up for a vacation. People oriented to long-range goals such as getting a higher degree are able to tolerate deprivations for years in the service of a larger aim. Delayed gratification can enhance our lives.

Desire

Psychologists have tried to categorize emotions into "families" based on a core emotion with its nuances and shades, but there is no agreement on which ones are basic. Fear, anger, sadness, and enjoyment have been proposed, as well as love, acceptance, surprise, disgust, and shame. According to Eastern philosophy, emotions are based on three reactions: attachment, aversion, or a neutral response. Desire is recognized as such a powerful element in emotional life that the Sanskrit word for the emotional nature is *kama*, "desire."

Most emotions fall into pairs based on attraction and aversion—love and hate, joy and sorrow, elation and depression. Such polarized emotions give a tinge of liking or disliking, pleasure or pain, to sensations. For example, as food preferences in different cultures show, the emotional reactions to the taste come from the brain and conditioning of the emotions, along with memories and thoughts involved with the sensations.

Motivation is a form of desire. If you want ice cream for dessert, you are motivated to go to the store to buy some. If you want to win at tennis, you practice often to master strategies. If you want to become a physician, you spend years studying and endure grueling days and nights on call at a hospital. Our motivation to achieve something we want is emotionally driven. It sets the direction of our lives. Our circumstances can be profoundly influenced by what we are motivated to work for. Desire is a basic element, not only in day-to-day experience, but in the larger shape of our lives.

Desire comes in many guises. We all have at least traces of purely selfish desire—greed, lust, ambition. We all hunger for things like food, comfort, and sex. Such desires are personified in Buddhist iconography as "hungry ghosts," beings with enormous bellies and pinhole mouths that can never take in enough to satisfy their endless appetites. These appetites include psychological longings for love and esteem. We also have unselfish desires—for a sick friend to get well, for better conditions in the inner city, for world peace, for saving the environment. Even the quest for enlightenment or union with the divine is based on desire.

Control of desire is one of our most difficult and necessary tasks, and our severest trials and suffering come from our struggle with our desirous nature. A large part of a spiritual life is purifying desire. Rather than being primarily motivated by desire for ourselves and our personal concerns, we gradually shift focus to others and to the general good, to altruism.

While Western psychology holds that emotional health requires the fulfillment of our needs and some desires, Buddhism holds that the most important virtue to cultivate is nonattachment to what is desirable. The Buddha taught that desire and clinging to the objects of desire bind us to the conditioned world with its ever-changing joys and suffering, thereby keeping us from peace and contentment. Desire, grasping, and clinging are the causes of suffering. Epictetus said, "If you want to make a man happy add not to his riches but take away from his desires" (Walsh and Vaughan 50).

Giving up desire seems colorless and austere to us. After all, the American dream is based on fulfilling desires. But we have all experienced the peace of not wanting anything. Recall a time when you felt completely satisfied. Nothing was lacking, and you were not striving for anything or expecting anything. You might have felt such fulfillment in quiet times in nature, after a beautiful concert, after a period of pleasant physical exertion such as a hike, after an intimate evening en rapport with someone you are close to, during meditation. You were content, wanting nothing. In such a non-grasping state, you can see things in perspective, unclouded by wants and extraneous emotions, and spiritual perception is possible.

According to the Indian and Tibetan traditions, desire has a powerful, long-lasting effect. They hold that our last desire at the time of death molds our after-death states and influences our next birth. The Brihadaranyaka Upanishad says, "We live in accordance with our deep, driving desire. It is this desire at the time of death that determines what our next life is to be" (Eswaran 48). But this last desire is not arbitrary or based on a temporary condition, such as an illness. It is the involuntary result of our desires, passions, and motivations during a whole lifetime. *The Mahatma Letters* advise that "it is for this very reason—that our last desire may not be unfavorable to our future progress—that we have to watch our actions and control our passions and desires throughout our whole earthly career" (326).

On the one hand, it is natural for us to be attracted or repulsed by most stimuli that we encounter. But thoughtless grasping and clinging to the pleasant and avoiding the unpleasant prevents freedom of choice by binding us to automatic reactions. On the other hand, we can learn to step back from desire for a moment and understand it, rather than being driven thoughtlessly by it. Though mind and emotion often work in harmony, the mind can distance itself from emotion and observe feelings without acting on them. Eventually unsatisfied desire weakens and dies out.

If one becomes skilled in practicing desirelessness, hunger, thirst, and other desires will still arise. But they are quickly satisfied without disturbing the background sense of contentment. One continues to act effectively in the world, but more spontaneously and without a sense of unrest or driving ambition.

The spiritual treatise *Light on the Path* advises:

Desire only that which is within you.
Desire only that which is beyond you.
Desire only that which is unattainable. (Collins 10)

In time we will all desire only atma, "The Self, pure awareness, [that] shines as the light within the heart" (Easwaran 43). We will then be free of restless yearning and at peace with our desires.

Empathy

For emotional health we need to be able to give and receive love and to forgive both ourselves and others. Empathy, the ability to sense others' emotions, is an important ingredient of loving relationships and of forgiveness. It is based on self-awareness, or being open to what we ourselves are feeling.

Emotions are rarely verbalized but are usually communicated through tone of voice, shift in posture, gesture, and facial expression. We ordinarily take in such clues unconsciously, but empathy requires that subtle signs be noticed. It can lead to rapport with others, to understanding their perspective, and a respect for reactions that are different from our own. Communication often breaks down, for example, between a parent and a teenager, because one person is upholding a point of view without trying to understand the other person's perspective. Greater awareness of another's feelings often reveals new solutions and promotes loving relations.

The ability to understand other people—what motivates them and how to work with them—is a large part of interpersonal intelligence, which correlates with intrapersonal intelligence, the ability to form a realistic model of oneself. Interpersonal intelligence can appear at a very young age (Goleman 36–37). Four-year-old Judy, at a preschool where various kinds of intelligence were taught, showed remarkable ability. The children were shown a dollhouse replica of their classroom, with each child represented by a stick figure with a photo of his or her head attached. With complete accuracy, Judy was able to put all the children in the part of the room where they most liked to play, and she grouped together figures representing those who were close friends. A keen observer of the social relations in her preschool classroom, she had sophisticated insights into other pupils. Some people like Judy have a talent for empathy and rapport, while others are emotionally "tone deaf." But we can all improve our ability to empathize by paying more attention to others' emotional expressions.

Breaking Patterns

Unconscious emotional patterns are insidious. They can migrate from generation to generation. You may have caught yourself sounding like your father scolding you when you scold your child, or you may disapprove of something innocuous your neighbor does, like hanging the wash in plain view of passers-by, without connecting your reaction with your mother's censure of her neighbors. Or you may respond in sympathy to big, blue-eyed blonds, a trait handed down from your brunette grandmother who was attached to her Swedish grandfather.

The power of habit and conditioning is illustrated in a bit of circus fiction that's fun to believe but not really true (Holst 21). In the early 1900s, two Alaskan kodiak bears were trained to dance on their hind legs, stepping in unison, paw in paw. They also turned somersaults and stood on their heads. Performing under bright spotlights at the circus, they became favorites of the crowds.

One year, the circus toured in South America. Off the coast of Chile in the southernmost islands of Tierra del Fuego, tragedy struck. A jaguar attacked the animal trainer and mauled him to death. In the confusion that followed, the bears escaped and were never found.

Seventy years later, scientists discovered a population of kodiak bears in the wilderness of several islands of Tierra del Fuego, where the climate and environment were just right for Alaskan bears. The scientists watched in amazement as they saw all the bears performing circus tricks. On bright moonlit nights, they gathered in a sparkling circular crater with white walls of chalk made glassy long ago by a meteorite. The white graveled floor was twice as bright as anywhere else in the vicinity. The bears rounded up the cubs and juveniles in a circle, and they all danced, paw in paw, stepping in unison! The scientists speculated that the brilliant light had reminded the original pair of the circus spotlight and they responded with their circus act.

Our conditioning is not as spectacular as this, and it is often negative and unproductive. But, like the bears, much of it is handed down from our parents, grandparents, and even distant fore-fathers, though we also build up conditioning in our own childhood and in later life as well.

Habitual emotions are hard to recognize. They are in the background of our consciousness and seem to be part of our nature. Yet they dominate us. They appear in the aura as more or less permanent patterns of color and energy that obstruct the aura's natural harmonious flow. An emotion like anger in the form of repressed resentment is very hard to deal with and can smolder for years, even for a lifetime. Such automatic negative habits cause trouble in our relations and in our lives, binding us to old reactions that may not be appropriate in the present. They do not express our best selves. Dora Kunz used to recommend to her students that, when they become aware of such a pattern, they take a deep breath and be still for a moment. You might do likewise and then say light-heartedly, "There I go again." That response frees you from the ingrained reaction so that you can face afresh whatever is before you.

Defusing Anger

Anger is a reaction often addressed by spiritual disciplines. It is a complex emotion in that it is almost always a secondary reaction derived from hurt, pain, jealousy, or a threat to one's ego. The goal in managing anger is not necessarily to get rid of it altogether but to channel it creatively. If handled wisely, anger can be effective in bringing about needed changes. Many important reforms, such as suffrage for women and equal rights for people of color, have been fueled by anger channeled into effective action. For it to be effective, however, we need to be able to express and communicate anger appropriately. Aristotle recognized this long ago when he said, "Anyone can become angry—that is easy. But to be angry at the right person, at the right time, for the right purpose, and in the right way—this is not easy" (Goleman 56). The skillful expression of anger takes place after we have cooled down and can talk rationally about what troubles us.

Because emotion is often touched off by thoughts, ruminating about what made you angry only increases the anger. Frances Vaughan and other therapists agree that ventilating anger is one of the worst ways to try to cool down because anger feeds on itself. Focusing the mind on something positive diverts the negative emotion. A Buddhist antidote for anger is to replace it with thoughts of loving-kindness. Dora Kunz advises us to acknowledge the feeling and say, "At this moment I am feeling angry" (179). Then take a deep breath and visualize a pleasant scene or someone you love. This may break the hold the emotion has on you.

Another useful method for handling anger is to reframe a disturbing situation in a more positive light. A study was done in which the experimenter was rude to the students who volunteered as subjects. Then the experimenter left the room, but another experimenter was present and heard the angry things they said about the first experimenter when he had gone. She told the students that he was under terrible pressure getting ready for his oral exams. When they next saw him, though he was still rude, they were no longer hostile toward him. Mitigating information changed their angry reactions. If you knew that the man who cut you off on the freeway was taking his wife to the hospital to deliver her baby, you might not have gotten angry. Such information undermines the convictions that fuel anger. Reframing has proved to be a very effective way to defuse angry reactions.

Jack Kornfield suggests reframing the ordinary difficulties of life by viewing them as a spiritual practice (*Path with Heart* 82). He teaches a meditation for changing the way you perceive difficulties. Picture the whole earth as filled with enlightened Buddhas. The only unenlightened being is you. Imagine that all the Buddhas are there to teach you. Whatever you encounter in life is just what you need to lead you toward enlightenment. Instead of resisting difficulties, you reframe them as opportunities for understanding and growth.

Disidentification

Ordinarily, we unconsciously identify with our emotions. We seldom separate ourselves from our needs, desires, and wishes but are driven by them. Although it is difficult to detach from an emotion and not be carried away by it, it is possible to train oneself to do so. Psychologists define "metacognition" as being aware of one's thoughts and "metamood" as being aware of one's emotions and feelings. Through our facility for self-consciousness, we can disengage from the energies of the aura or "astral body" and observe and analyze them. We can act as an observer of what goes on within our consciousness. The very act of watching emotions helps to break the habit of identifying with them. In the act of watching, the emotions being watched do not exist alone; there is also the "I" who watches.

Roberto Assagioli gives his patients exercises to help them disidentify from their emotions so that they are no longer their victims. You say to yourself, "I *have* emotions but I *am not* my emotions" (*Psychosynthesis* 116–18). When you feel irritated, for example, you allow yourself to experience the irritation. But instead of saying, "I am irritated," and identifying yourself with irritation, you say, "There is in me a state of irritation." You acknowledge the emotion while realizing that it is not a permanent condition.

Furthermore, you see that the "I" is not the irritation. The "I" is "simple, unchanging, constant self-consciousness" and could be formulated as "I am I, a center of pure consciousness." Assagioli teaches other affirmations too: "I always remain I, *myself*, in times of hope or of despair, in joy or in pain, in a state of irritation or calm. . . . I recognize and affirm myself as a center of pure self-consciousness." Such practices lead to the realization that emotions, like the body and mind, are instruments of experience. They are changeable and impermanent. They can be dominated and used by the "I," whose nature as pure consciousness is something entirely different from them.

Making affirmations is not the same as experiencing atma, but they can help us break our identity with our emotions. Affirmations can implant the knowledge that the personality is not the whole of us and can point us in the direction of a firsthand experience of atma.

Emotions, like thoughts and sensations, are the inevitable result of activating one of our principles and its vehicle—kama and the emotional field. Emotions are unavoidable. But if we know who we are and what our relationship is to those emotions as they rise and fall, we remain the silent atma, the background consciousness on which they play. The ancient seer who composed the Brihadaranyaka Upanishad said of a person in union with the Self or atma that "in the unitive state all desires find their perfect fulfillment. There is no other desire that needs to be fulfilled, and one goes beyond sorrow" (Eswaran 45). In that state of deep peace, all desire dies in the light of the One Life. We taste *ananda*, the joy inherent in atma, which is not dependent on any condition.

Chapter 5

The Mind:
Bipolar Consciousness

*The human mind is not only the most wonderful thing in cre-
ation but also the greatest problem of the man who is trying to
tread the path to perfection and Enlightenment.*

I. K. Taimni

Brian is a freelance science writer. He studies a subject such as gla-
ciers, black holes, or brain chemistry and produces lively, readable
articles and books. He is good at what he does. He looks for underlying principles that give shape and meaning to scattered data. He
is good at analyzing information and coming up with logical conclusions. Even in making personal decisions, such as buying a car,
he gathers information and analyzes it to find the best choice for
him. He seldom skips a step in a logical sequence. His office is
orderly, with his source books arranged in the most efficient way.
Even his drawers and closet are neat and organized, as is his daily
routine and schedule. He has an impersonal point of view in his
writing and in life in general and tends to be unbiased and objective
in his approach to everything. When settling his children's arguments,

as when negotiating with an editor, he is impartial and fair. He is not swayed by what appeals to him at the moment but only what is best for the situation.

Brian is quiet, reserved, and a bit shy. It is hard to draw him into conversation, as he is often preoccupied with his current project rather than with those around him. He does not need or want much social life, and he is ill at ease with small talk. He has one-pointed interest in his work, and emotions and relationships are much less important to him. His wife tells him that he is sometimes unemotional and detached.

Brian would be classified as a thinking type and an introvert on the Myers-Briggs Type Indicator. As a thinking type, he is objective and task-oriented, as well as logical and impersonal, not primarily concerned with the way he affects people. However, not all thinking types are concerned with intellectual pursuits. Typically, surgeons and judges are thinking types, as are many ordinary people from all walks of life. Henry Ford was a thinking type, in that because he applied underlying principles to his field of making and marketing automobiles. Brian is an introvert because his primary focus is on internal concerns, not on the world and people around him.

Mental Functions

Brian is good with many of the functions of the mind that we use everyday. Most of these are concerned with structuring and ordering our experience. When you think, "The next step is . . ." or "If . . . then . . ." or "This goes there . . ." or "That adds up to . . ." or "My conclusion is . . . ," you are using mental functions. When you make a schedule for the day, balance your checkbook, give someone directions to the post office, follow a recipe, or come to a logical conclusion, you are exercising your mind. In these mundane mental tasks, you are manipulating and giving structure to individual items—images, thoughts, ideas. Common functions of the mind are discrimination, comparison, judgment, logic, contrasting, reasoning, sorting. Scientific knowledge, the result of mental functions, gives shape and structure to human experience. It has been compared to a beautiful crystalline structure growing in the amorphous mass of raw experience. Philosophy also serves this function. The mind can give meaning to experience, and meaning is a necessary ingredient for a healthy orientation to life.

In concrete thinking, your mind sees the world as composed of discrete, concrete items. This level of the mind has been called the concrete, empirical, or separative mind. The mind also has an abstract function that deals with generalities and universals encompassing many concrete instances in their scope (chapter 2). You have seen any number of triangles, each of a particular size, color, and shape. You know that a right triangle drawn in blue and an isosceles triangle drawn in black are both triangles. You may even have learned to prove it by logical steps. Your concept of a triangle as a three-sided figure does not depend on any particular size, shape, or color. Concepts like "triangle" are universal generalities that include all instances. Handling universals is a function of the abstract mind, sometimes called the higher mind, though it is higher only in the sense of being more inclusive, not of being better. Advanced mathematics and philosophy are characteristic of the higher mind.

Thoughts Shape the World

In the West, we prize logical thought. Our educational system is largely based on developing the rational function of the mind, although other modes of education are also practiced. Since logic is at the heart of the scientific method, and we place high value on science, logic colors our understanding of what the mind is. But thought and the mind are much more deep-seated than their conscious functions of logical thinking and solving problems with reason. The way we view the world, our actions and attitudes, our health, and our orientation to life are all shaped by what we think.

The profound influence of thought on a global level is illustrated in the opening of the preamble to the United Nations charter: "Since wars begin in the minds of men. . . ." Jiddu Krishnamurti pointed out that people's attitudes and beliefs divided them psychologically. The border between Russia and Iran is an example of artificial division. There are no buildings or population for miles around the crossing point. Yet spanning a dried-up riverbed is a bridge with a gate at its middle, locked on both sides. To pass between the two countries, travelers must walk to the gate, show their papers, wait for the guard to unlock the gate, walk through it, and show the papers to the guard on the other side.

Centuries-old conflicts as well as passing squabbles flow from the idea that the differences between one group and another are of paramount importance. Although geographic and cultural differences mark two peoples, for example, Palestinians and Israelis, what really divides them is mental and emotional. Wars are fought over beliefs, ideas, and attachments that exist only in the mind. Belief acts like a material force in the world. Thomas Jefferson said that any change in laws and institutions must be accompanied by progressive development of the human mind.

The stock market is another example of something driven by attitudes and beliefs. People buy and sell stocks and bonds, depending on the ideas generated by the day's news. Market fluctuations ride on the prevailing attitude of traders that day.

The very way we experience the world is shaped by our ideas and expectations. In one of Charles Schultz's "Peanuts" comic strips,

Lucy, Linus (the intellectual), and Charlie Brown are lying on a hillside gazing up at cloud formations. Lucy asks Linus what he sees up there. He says, "That cloud on the left looks like a map of British Honduras. The cloud in the center reminds me of a bust by the famous artist Thomas Eakins. The cloud on the right shows the stoning of Stephen; you can see St. Paul standing there." Lucy asks Charlie Brown what he sees in the clouds. He tells her, "I was going to say that I saw a horsie and a duckie, but I changed my mind." Like Linus and Charlie Brown, what we perceive as the actual world, not just in cloud pictures, depends on what is in our minds. The philosopher Immanuel Kant pointed out this fact when he said that the mind is an active, forming participant in what it knows.

In a similar vein, a Tibetan teacher once drew a loose V on the board in front of his class and asked the students what it was. They interpreted it as a picture of a bird drawn cartoon style. To the teacher it was a picture of the sky with a bird flying in it. The students got a lesson in looking for the spiritual background behind the world of forms.

We do not realize how much our worldview and our cultural biases affect what we perceive and how our language and logic mold our thought processes. For instance, the Theosophist and linguist Benjamin Lee Whorf pointed out that many of us perceive snow either as white and fluffy or as packed, whereas the Eskimos have many words for snow that denote how hard or soft, icy or runny it is, so they perceive many nuances of its condition that we miss. Whorf's major statement of his ideas about how our language influences the way we think and even the way we see things was first published in the *American Theosophist* magazine and later by the MIT Press in a collection of his writings, *Language, Thought, and Reality*. He observed that we look at the world as made up primarily of static things such as houses and trees, but the Hopi language tends to regard the world as consisting of processes that are constantly in a state of change. Similarly, Sanskrit has words to describe many meditative states. We have no language for these states, so may come to the conclusion that they do not exist. Our language is a filter of reality.

Even our senses show us only a particular version of reality. Our vision and hearing respond only within a certain range of frequencies. We do not see infrared as snakes do or ultraviolet as bees can. Dogs hear high frequencies that do not register in our brains. Because objects we see and sense seem so real "out there," it is hard to realize that they are only images in our minds, not outer reality in itself.

Unconscious Thought Patterns

In addition to the limitations of our language and our senses, we each develop partly unconscious patterns of thinking and feeling that color our perception and our responses. For instance, think of someone you love or someone you strongly dislike. Does your mental perception evoke love and affection? Or anger and aversion? Your reaction to that person may depend on a recent happy time with her or a bitter argument, or it may be colored by a long-standing attitude of love and trust or by fear, hostility, and distrust. Especially habitual thoughts, feelings, and attitudes carve grooves in our minds, creating prejudices, beliefs, likes and dislikes, divisions, preconceptions, conditioned responses, and stereotypes—individual and cultural.

This is how our conditioning distorts our view of reality, as a mirror in the fun house distorts the images it reflects. H. P. Blavatsky's spiritual guidebook *The Voice of the Silence* says, "The mind is the slayer of the Real. Let the disciple slay the slayer" (1). She does not, of course, mean for us to stop using our minds but to be aware of the way they distort our perception of reality. I. K. Taimni explains that our prejudices and rigid ideas interfere with free circulation of the matter in our mental fields and impede our ability to think clearly and correctly (100). As the patterns repeat themselves and block out new insight, they interfere with our contact with things as they really are.

Character and Thought Patterns

We create, not just our views of others, but even our own character by what we think and feel habitually. For as Frances Vaughan points out, "Many spiritual teachings, East and West, tell us that we shape ourselves and our world with our thoughts" (*Shadows of the Sacred* 154). Do you have a tendency toward irritation or toward cheerfulness? You may have noticed that the more you react in either way, the stronger the tendency becomes. Annie Besant explains that thought affects the very stuff of which our mental bodies are composed. The effect is so powerful that "every quiver of consciousness, though it be due only to a passing thought, draws into the mental body some particles of mind-stuff, and shakes out other particles from it" (*Thought Power* 31).

We may even come to think that our tendencies of mind and emotion are ourselves and that we cannot change them. But these conditioned ways of reacting are only a small part of us. We have many other tendencies and principles in our nature that are not involved in these particular reactions at all. Ultimately, we are the consciousness that can become aware of and detached from conditioned responses, thus letting them die out for lack of fuel.

Mind-Body Interaction

Try this experiment to see the interaction between your body and your mind. Close your eyes and think of lifting a heavy box. Using your imagination, bend your knees to take the strain off your back. Now notice how your body feels. Did your muscles tighten as though you were really lifting a weight? Now with eyes closed, visualize a lemon. Imagine yourself getting a knife and cutting it in half. Squeeze some juice into a cup and smell it. Are you salivating?

The field of mind-body medicine, which demonstrates the interaction between these two aspects of ourselves, has become well known through the work of physicians and researchers like Bernie Siegel, Larry Dossey, Andrew Weil, Deepak Chopra, Jeanne Achterberg, and Joan Borysenko.

Larry Dossey begins his book *Space, Time and Medicine* by relating a bizarre incident that happened when he was an intern (3–6). An elderly man in the hospital was dying. He had lost fifty pounds in six months and was profoundly weak, almost bedfast. Yet nothing in his numerous X-rays and blood tests showed anything wrong, and no explanation could be found for the illness. Dossey's friend and companion intern, Jim, told this to the patient. The old man said, "I know why I am dying." It turned out that the man, who believed in voodoo, had been hexed by a shaman hired by an enemy. The shaman had gotten a lock of the patient's hair from his wife, which was used for the hex. The victim never doubted the effectiveness of the hex and accepted his death as an accomplished fact. He lost so much of his will to live that he refused to eat.

Jim, however, did not accept the impending death. He and Dossey cooked up a plan. Late one night on a weekend, when there was little traffic in the hospital, they rolled the dying man in a wheelchair into an examining room that was dark except for the eerie light of a blue flame burning in an ashtray. Jim took on a shaman-like demeanor. He snipped a lock of the patient's hair and told him that he was going to burn the hair in the flame and that as it burned the hex would be destroyed. He made the patient swear that he would never speak of this ceremony to anyone (partly to save himself from ridicule by skeptical hospital personnel).

The next morning, the patient awoke with a voracious appetite. He ate three breakfasts and double lunches and dinners. He was cheerful and his weight increased dramatically. Jim kept him in the hospital for a few days, then released him. Neither mentioned the midnight "ceremony." This man's belief had almost killed him, and it also saved him.

Health and the Mind

The mind affects the body profoundly, even without a conscious choice, such as refusing to eat. There is extensive evidence that beliefs, attitudes, and emotions affect both acute and chronic diseases and can bring about physical changes in heart rate, blood pressure, respiration, blood sugar, white cell count, muscle potential, skin temperature, hormone secretion, brain waves, and gastrointestinal activity. For example, in his book *Meaning and Medicine*, Dossey reports on the "black Monday syndrome" (62–63). Studies show that there are more heart attacks on Monday than on any other day of the week. Even more striking is the fact that they cluster around 8:00 and 9:00 AM, the time the workweek begins after the weekend. Furthermore, the best predictor of a first heart attack is not high blood pressure, elevated cholesterol level, smoking, or diabetes. It is dissatisfaction with one's job.

On the other hand, among ambitious, successful people who are highly motivated in their jobs, those who are "type A," with a continual inward sense of urgency and pressure, have a higher mortality rate from heart disease and die earlier than "type B" people, who are more relaxed and less driven. The science of psychoneuroimmunology, which studies the relation between inner states and the immune system, clearly shows that worry, overwork, and anxiety can damage the immune system. Stress can lead to anything from headache to heart disease and can even be fatal.

You may have discovered that you don't usually get sick when your mental state is positive and you are relaxed and free from stress. Positive attitudes, beliefs, and emotions are known to improve health. "Consciousness therapies" are based on knowledge of mind-body connections. One such therapy is biofeedback, in which you learn to control usually unconscious functions such as heart rate and blood pressure. Many relaxation techniques have also been developed (Emery 63). In one, you alternately tense and relax muscles. You begin by inhaling and curling your toes tightly as you hold your breath. You then exhale as you relax toes and feet. Then repeat the whole sequence. You work your way up to your face and scalp by tensing and relaxing different parts of your body. Such exercises are very helpful for relieving stress.

In autogenic training, you teach the body to respond to suggestion. In one technique, you learn the "relaxation response" by training yourself to relax in response to a silently repeated word you choose, such as "relax" or "peace." Then when you are in a stressful situation, you repeat the word. Your automatic response is to relax, so you stay calm rather than tensing up and increasing stress.

Numerous studies have shown that meditation has pronounced physical effects. For example, Transcendental Meditation has been shown to lower elevated blood cholesterol levels, and so does just sitting quietly in a chair for twenty minutes twice a day (Dossey, *Space, Time and Medicine* 63). Physicians refer patients with various kinds of diseases to yoga and meditation programs, often sponsored by hospitals and clinics. Therapies like these, as well as activities like listening to soothing music, exercising, and playing, release endorphins in the brain that circulate throughout the body. We might think of them as "happiness chemicals" that create good feelings and promote health.

The mental activity of imaging works for relaxation and stress reduction, but it can do much more. In a well-known pioneer study, along with conventional medical therapy and lifestyle changes, Carl and Stephanie Simonton had medically incurable cancer patients spend time each day visualizing their white blood cells attacking cancer cells. Of the original group, their results showed that 22 percent of the patients showed no evidence of disease and in 19 percent the tumor was regressing. Those who died lived one-and-a-half times as long as was expected (Simonton and Creighton 11–12). This study has been replicated, and the technique is used by many doctors and therapists. Some patients think up creative and colorful imagery, such as fierce sharks attacking the cancer cells. One little boy in a later study developed a computer-like war game. The same technique has been tried by people with colds and found to increase the cells that fight the infection. The "Mother Teresa effect" is also effective in aborting colds. If you think you have a cold coming on, relax while you think of a time when you felt deeply loved and also a time when you felt love for another person. Studies show that your cold probably won't develop (Dossey, *Healing Words* 109–10). Deliberately directed thoughts and feelings have powerful effects on the body.

Distant Effects of Thought

Convincing evidence shows that our thoughts, like our emotions, are nonlocal and can affect others at a distance (chapters 2 and 4). At some time, you probably have known who the caller was before you picked up the phone. You have probably had the experience of staring at the back of someone's head and seeing him turn around toward you. Rupert Sheldrake has investigated such experiences (Sheldrake, "Experiments").

It is not uncommon for people to know of an injury to or the death of a distant loved one before they get the news. A striking example is a case involving three women. One had the strong impression that her mother was seriously ill and needed her. Against her husband's advice, she hurried to the mother's house. As she approached, she met her sister who had gotten the same impression about her mother and was also coming to see her. It turned out that the mother was dying and had been asking to see her daughters (Dossey, *Healing Words* 53).

"Telesomatic" events are even stronger indications of the influence of thought at a distance. In such cases, a physical event affecting one person is simultaneously felt by another person who is far away. For example, a woman awoke one morning at 7:00, feeling a blow to her lip so hard that she looked for blood. Later that morning, her husband came in holding a handkerchief to his bleeding lip. He had gone out on his boat early that morning. At 7:00 AM, the tiller had swung in a gust of wind, hitting him hard in the mouth. In another case, a woman suddenly doubled over as though in severe pain, saying that something had happened to her friend, Nell. Two hours later, the sheriff came to tell her that Nell had been in an automobile accident; part of the steering wheel had penetrated her chest. She died on the way to the hospital (Dossey, *Healing Words* 50).

Our Mental Field

Clairvoyant investigations provide other views of the reality of thought and its influence on ourselves and others. In addition to our emotional field, we each have a personal mental field fashioned from the subtle stuff of the universal mental field and responding to its energies (as discussed in chapter 2). Consciousness is unlimited in itself; however, in the physical world, it works through its vehicles, including the mental body and the brain. In their book *Thought Forms*, Annie Besant and C. W. Leadbeater described the effect of thoughts in the superphysical matter of the mental field. They observed radiating vibratory energy and floating forms of various colors and shapes as thoughts arose in the aura of a thinker. If the thought is fleeting, the thought form is fleeting; if strong, it persists for a longer period. These forms often hover around their creator and are reinforced by new thoughts that resonate with the original impulse. Thus, strong patterns are built up and become very hard to change. We become enclosed, as it were, in a cage of our own building (10).

The energy of thought forms works through the vital body to affect physical functions. Patterns of repeated thought and feeling can enhance or impede the normal flow of prana in the body (as shown in chapter 3). For instance, constant worry can affect the adrenal glands and the immune system and thus result in disease. Medical clairvoyants are able to perceive these patterns and can sometimes diagnose illusive causes of illness, even before physical symptoms develop.

As with emotions, we continuously affect others by our thoughts, and in turn we are affected by the thoughts of others. Like emotions, thought forms can move across the mental field and reverberate in those who receive them. A mother's repeated prayers for the protection of her child can affect the child, as can repeated thoughts of resentment or ill will toward someone. A strong thought of love and good will or of jealousy and resentment directed at someone strengthens that tendency in him or her. Our thoughts are not merely subjective and private. As *The Mahatma Letters* tell us, "Thoughts are things—have tenacity, coherence, and life . . . they are real entities" (49).

We exercise this immense unconscious power of thought all the time. We can learn to use it consciously for the good of ourselves and others by deliberately sending positive thoughts and images of healing, peace, and good will to others and to difficult situations.

Teilhard de Chardin recognized the power of inner states when he said, "The day will come, after harnessing space, the winds, the tides, and gravitation, we shall harness for God the energies of love. And on that day, for the second time in the history of the world, we shall have discovered fire."

Mind and Consciousness

According to Theosophy, our minds, like consciousness, are not really our own. Consciousness is universal and not confined to one place or time, but works in all the fields that make up the world, which includes us. Similarly, *manas,* the Sanskrit term for the faculty of cognition, is a specialized aspect of universal consciousness that has as its vehicles both our mental field and brain. Thoughts affect the mental part of our aura, our mental field.

Consciousness seems to get trapped in our brains and nervous systems. This gives us a sense of ourselves as being separated from the whole. Yet our individual consciousness and its modification in manas are truly cosmic, not limited in time and space, but stepped-down versions of universal consciousness. The thinking principle in us resonates with universal mind. As Blavatsky noted, "Mahat or the 'universal mind' is the source of Manas [the human mind]" (*Key to Theosophy* 135). Looked at in this way, the effects of thought at a distance seem natural.

Mind over Matter

You may have experienced thoughts that make things happen in the physical world. Have you ever "manifested" a parking space by visualizing it? Imagery and visualization can affect the growth of fungi and the outcome of events in a random event generator. Such use of thought power, or psychokinesis, is many steps from learning to manifest whatever you want, as taught by some schools of thought.

But attracting something can also be done in a natural, untutored way. For instance, nine-year-old Sally saw her beloved dog run over and killed, and of course she was heartbroken. She prayed hard for a new puppy that night. A strange little dog appeared on her front lawn the next morning. The girl's parents insisted on trying to find the owners. They advertised and spread the word, but no one claimed the dog, so Sally got to keep it. Did the unhappy child attract the new puppy by the strength of her thought?

Jack Kornfield, who teaches Buddhist meditation, illustrates the power of the mind with a story from the East ("Take One Seat"). It seems that a seeker wandered from place to place to find happiness. One day, exhausted from his search, he sat under a tree to rest. Unwittingly, he chose a wish-fulfilling tree. He thought it was a lovely spot and that he would like to have a small house there. Immediately, a pretty cottage appeared. Then he thought it would be nice to have a wife to share the house with him. Suddenly a lovely woman was there, smiling at him shyly. He felt hungry and wished for something to eat. A serving cart appeared before him with delicious dishes. As he leaned back on the tree contentedly, he began to wonder what was going on. He decided that there must be some kind of a demon living in the tree, and with that a demon appeared before him. The frightened wanderer thought, "Oh, he's going to eat me!" And that is just what the demon did!

Dualistic Thought

Kornfield's story is a parable about the creative power of the mind, but it illustrates another prominent feature of the thinking process. The discriminative or lower mind separates the observer from what is observed. The seeker in the story saw the house, wife, and demon as outside of himself, though we are apt to interpret them as within his own mind. We, too, feel ourselves to be different from our mental creations, which are images or ideas in our minds. The fact that we can stand aside from ideas and manipulate them mentally through symbols allows for abstract thinking. This ability, an aspect of self-consciousness, is the source of language, mathematics, music, and art.

The human mind is the greatest achievement of evolution on our planet. In our lifetime we have put a man on the moon, split the atom, unraveled the secrets of heredity and DNA, and even cloned animals. Throughout history, we have produced magnificent paintings and music and created literature that inspires us. We have conceived of the Magna Carta and the American Constitution, as well as many other styles of governing ourselves and regulating our societies. Accomplishments in art, literature, science, philosophy, religion, and technology in cultures throughout the ages are overwhelming in their totality. In every field and every age, the human mind, through its capacity for language, writing, and mathematics, has revolutionized our world, both externally and internally. Throughout history, the mind has continued to evoke new dimensions and depths of experience, and it will continue to do so.

Yet, the process of thinking and naming things, while it gives us great power, cuts us off from reality. Thinking is dualistic: the mind deals in thoughts and concepts about the objects of thought, not directly with the objects themselves, and experiences itself as different from the object it thinks about. Dualistic thought is incapable of knowing reality first hand. Like the chemist who analyzes the chemical composition of water rather than experiencing its coolness, taste, or transparency, we experience our mental processes *about* a thing rather than knowing the thing directly. Plato's allegory of the cave depicts this situation. In that story, people are chained to their seats, facing the back wall of a cave. They see only the shadows on the wall cast by other people moving between a fire and the mouth of the cave. In this position, the cave dwellers can never see reality, only shadows that are incomplete and distorted replicas, like the representations of reality in our minds.

Self-Consciousness

Dualistic thinking is associated with self-consciousness, which is the ability to know oneself as a center of individual awareness. Ever since you were a small child, you have known that "this is me," that your brother or the family dog is not yourself. You can see yourself as different and apart from what you are thinking about. Therefore, you can step aside from the immediate problem, consider alternate solutions, and decide what action to take. Your ability to observe your own mind and differentiate it from your thoughts allows you to make deliberate decisions, and it also allows you to learn from experience and correct yourself. A mountain lion would not think over the kill he just made and concoct a strategy for doing better next time. Self-consciousness and the ability for symbolic representation and self-examination make us responsible for what we do. Blavatsky says that self-consciousness is a hallmark of being human. It is also the root of some important human characteristics such as dealing in symbols, which makes possible language, mathematics, and planning for the future, as mentioned earlier.

Self-consciousness is a huge step in evolution. Yet it, along with dualistic thinking, is responsible for the greatest impediment to ultimate spiritual insight. That impediment is feeling ourselves to be distinct, separate selves. We unconsciously divide the universe into two categories, ourselves and everything else. Thus, we see ourselves as apart from the "outer world" and from each other, and even apart from our own thoughts and feelings. Self-consciousness leads to the sense of being a distinct, separate self apart from the whole of things. Thus is born the ego, part of being human but the source of our greatest distortionsn (see chapter 8). The Indian sage Aurobindo said that you have to get out of the middle of the picture in order to see.

Self-consciousness need not be separative. The Buddha, for example, remained aware of himself as an individual long after his enlightenment experience, which dissolved any self-centeredness or self-interest apart from the whole. Unlike the Buddha's nonattachment to the personal self, the ego tends to consider everything from its particular point of view and related to its own limited concerns. In "The Marriage of Heaven and Hell," William Blake put this idea poetically:

> If the doors of perception were cleansed everything would appear to man as it is, infinite.
>
> For man has closed himself up, till he sees all things through narrow chinks of his cavern.

According to Theosophy, focus on separateness and self-concern is a necessary step in evolution. We evolve from an oceanic sense of homogeneous oneness to a sharp focus of distinct individuality (as mentioned in chapters 1 and 8). Then we return to the realization of oneness, but now with individualized self-consciousness, not ego consciousness. But the ego resists the movement toward unity and its own eventual demise. The aspect of the mind that creates ego and separateness is the most critical problem on the spiritual path. Of course, we must take care of ourselves and pay attention to personal concerns, but the challenge is to do this without losing a sense of partaking in universal life.

The Holistic Mind

The dualistic, analytical, discursive aspect of our minds is sometimes called the "lower" mind, though "lower" is not a term of value; it is only lower in the sense that low C is lower than high C on the piano. There is, however, another level of mind that is not characterized by dualism, though it operates at levels below the ultimate sense of unity with all, which the buddhic or intuitive faculty achieves (see chapter 6). Yet this octave of cognition, the higher mind, is integrative and holistic. Rather than focusing on particulars, it focuses on universals. Rather than analyzing into parts, it synthesizes and sees wholes. For example, a scientist might study separate aspects and specifics of the diet and digestive system of chimpanzees, or, like Jane Goodall, live with them in the wild, holistically empathizing with and studying their overall way of life. Charles Darwin and Alfred Wallace took an even broader view. Rather than focusing on detailed studies of individual species, they saw the grand scheme by which species are related to one another. Though Darwinian evolutionary theory has since shown weaknesses in its explanations, the overall grasp of the principle of the evolution of species was a penetrating insight that changed our culture's worldview.

Two Poles of the Mind

Thus, mind or *manas* has two poles, both necessary for functioning in the world as a complete human being. H. P. Blavatsky explained: "There is a spiritual consciousness, the Manasic mind illumined by the light of Buddhi [intuition], that which subjectively perceives abstractions, and the sentient consciousness (the lower Manasic light), inseparable from our physical brain and senses" (*Key to Theosophy* 179). The lower mind is part of the personality and gravitates toward particulars, often of personal concern. It anchors the self in the concrete, practical world. The higher mind, as part of the transpersonal self or soul, focuses on wholes and releases consciousness into a wider, transpersonal sphere that is closer to the One.

Directed toward the personal life, the mind confines us within our conception of being a separated self. Directed toward the realm of the One, it frees us from the confines of the ego and lifts us into a perspective of unity and wholeness that is large-minded and altruistic. Thus the mind partakes of both the personality and the transpersonal Self. Its function of dividing and making distinctions creates the separative ego; its function of perceiving wholes and relations guides us to the transpersonal self and the One. According to the Maitri Upanishad, "The mind is indeed the source of bondage, and also the source of liberation" (Mascaro 104).

The view from the transpersonal perspective is not limited to personal concerns but encompasses the total environment, physical and psychic. Ken Wilber says that "transpersonal" means "those realities that include, but go beyond the personal and the individual" ("To See a World" 149). He describes transpersonal concerns as "wider currents that sweep across the skin-encapsulated ego and touch other beings, touch the cosmos, touch spirit, touch patterns and places kept secret [from] those who hug the surfaces and surround themselves with themselves." Blavatsky also refers to a transpersonal breadth of vision: "Spiritual and divine powers lie dormant in every human Being; and the wider the sweep of his spiritual vision the mightier will be the God within him" (*Key to Theosophy* 181). The transpersonal goes beyond but also includes the personal.

A character in Longfellow's "The Song of Hiawatha" captures the double nature of the mind. In this poem, which is based on the traditions of the indigenous tribes who lived alongside the Great Lakes, the character called Mischief Maker is self-centered, proud, and cunning, and causes a great deal of trouble. He provokes Hiawatha by suggesting a game to the men of their particular tribe and then winning all their wampum, garments, feathers, and weapons. He taunts the great chief by strangling Raven, whirling him around like a rattle, and hanging the body from the ridgepole of the lodge. Next, he taunts the elders by throwing the lodge into wild disorder, piling up bowls, earthen kettles, buffalo robes, and other beautiful skins, then running away. Hiawatha and the other men hunt down the troublemaker and kill him. But Hiawatha, representing the divine spark or atma, resurrects him. Thereafter, the former Mischief Maker lives forever in a higher form as the great Pau-Puk-Keewis, who flies high over Hiawatha's head and guides him on his journeys, warning him of dangers. Thus, he grows from the level of the tricky, selfish lower mind to that of higher intelligence and guide.

Desire and Thought

We all must learn to function in both the personal and the transpersonal spheres. To do so, we need to gain control of the lower mind, which is usually driven by desires (though hopefully not for destructive naughtiness like Mischief Maker). The power of desire over the lower mind is illustrated by an episode in the comic strip "Rose Is Rose," which is based on the interaction between Rose and her three-year-old son, Pasquale.

One day Pasquale walks happily along with no thoughts on his mind (the balloon over his head in which words usually appear is empty). Suddenly, a chocolate sundae pops into the balloon. Next he is in the kitchen with Rose, who is saying, "Just stop *thinking* about a chocolate sundae." Pasquale walks away with a blank balloon. Suddenly half a sundae breaks into one side of the balloon. With a look of sheer determination, he pushes it out till the balloon goes blank again. But soon the complete sundae is prominently in the middle of the balloon. "Aaugh!" he says.

Soon Pasquale is in the kitchen again, saying to Rose, "Don't inka bowt chayrees troodle!" A serving of cherry strudel jumps halfway into Rose's balloon. "Nngh, nngh!" she says. Next we see them at a lunch counter, enjoying their favorite delicacies. Pasquale has a little loving heart above his head. Rose is saying, "Don't *ever* tell me not to think about cherry strudel."

We experience the strong resonance between the mind and desire every day. If you examine the thoughts streaming through your mind, you will soon become aware of how often they are motivated by desire and emotion. It is difficult to control them by the force of will or determination. In the Bhagavad Gita, Sri Krishna, representing the highest spirit and intelligence, agrees with Arjuna, the personality, that the mind is as hard to curb as the wind (6:33–36). But, he continues, it can be curbed by constant practice and by dispassion. Regular mental training and meditation can eventually calm the restlessness of the mind, so that it becomes at least temporarily free from desire, fear, and automatic thinking, and its powers can be directed as you will.

Meditation and Concentration

To curb the mind, we need to develop concentration and one-pointedness. There are many different types of meditation that do this. We will consider two types, one that is oriented toward calming and controlling the lower mind, the other toward developing the higher mind.

Both Annie Besant and I. K. Taimni offer many suggestions for exercises and practices to strengthen and control the lower mind. For example, to learn to concentrate, choose an object such as a flower, a crystal, or a peaceful scene in nature. Or you might prefer a devotional object or symbol, such as the cross, an image of Christ or the Buddha, or a mandala. Visualize it in as much detail as possible, holding your mind on the image. Besant advises looking at the object, closing your eyes and visualizing it, then with open eyes comparing your inner picture with the actual object (*Thought Power* 55). Careful observation sharpens and clarifies the mind.

A traditional Buddhist method to learn concentration is just to be mindful of your breath for a time. Your posture should be pleasant and easy and your back straight. Close your eyes and just pay attention to your inhalations and exhalations. Some traditions recommend counting each in-and-out cycle up to ten, then starting over again at one.

This simple exercise is surprisingly hard to do until the mind begins to be tamed. You will no doubt at times find thoughts intruding and your mind wandering. In the beginning, you may feel that your mind is more restless than ever. This is probably due to the fact that you have become far more aware of its movements than you were before. It is best just to let the thoughts flow past, as clouds float through the sky, and quietly bring your mind back to the breath again and again. Any feeling of annoyance or guilt interferes with the meditation. You should remain alert and awake and not fall into a trance-like state. In such a state, you are not training the mind, and the brain does not register your experience. It is wise to limit the practice to five or ten minutes in the beginning, building up to fifteen or twenty minutes and eventually half an hour. If you feel tension in your muscles or start to get a headache, then you should stop and relax for a time. It is important to know when your body is becoming tense while practicing.

Other practices focus on being mindful or aware of thoughts and feelings as they arise. This leads to greater awareness of our total inner state. We also become more aware of what is around us in the environment and of other people. Ideally, we learn to live in a state of global mindfulness of all that is in our consciousness—whether it arises from inner states or from outside—and our reactions to what is happening. There are many fine manuals on such practices, for example Joseph Goldstein's *The Experience of Insight* (Boulder: Shambhala, 1983).

The above practices are aimed at clearing the mind and being aware of the emotions, thoughts, and bodily sensations without lapsing into automatic reactions. Mindfulness thus leads to Roberto Assagioli's "disidentification" (see chapter 4), which has been called "objectifying the mind." After you have made a practice of observing the movements of your mind and have become familiar with its tendencies and characteristics, you come to realize that you are the observer—the consciousness—not the fleeting contents that pass through your mind. Through realizing that you are not the stream of thoughts of the personality, you can begin to identify with a deeper dimension. Then, at an even higher stage of insight, you realize that the observer and what is observed are parts of the same unity consciousness. The subject and object are one. This kind of awareness is a major theme for Jiddu Krishnamurti. From the Theosophical perspective, it leads to transpersonal awareness. "Our inmost Self, our ultimate Being, is Awareness itself, boundless, timeless, and spaceless," as put by Upanishadic scholar J. C. Chatterji (18).

To establish this new perspective, we need to practice withdrawing from the personal and entering into an inner quietude again and again until it becomes a persistent habit. The power of thought at this higher level is far greater than at lower levels. Cultivating the higher mind enhances our own journey to enlightenment, and by using the power of thought at this level, we can help to lift the thought atmosphere of the world.

A side effect of practices like those in the paragraphs above is an ability to drop things that worry you so that you can get a calmer perspective on them. These practices inhibit the modifications of the thinking principle, as the Indian sage Patanjali put it, which is necessary in the practice of Yoga.

There are forms of meditation meant to strengthen powers of the higher mind. Blavatsky, speaking of true spiritual wisdom or *jnana,* says that it "can only be attained by seeking to become *en rapport* with the Universal Soul (Atman)," but that one cannot be brought into communication with atman except through buddhi-manas, through the higher mind illumined by intuition (*Collected Writings* 12:634).

Jnana Yoga, one of the four traditional forms of Yoga that Blavatsky held is the Yoga for the West, leads to liberation through knowledge or wisdom of the higher mind. This Yoga is for those who like to explore and investigate, who are drawn to study. The jnana yogi explores worldly knowledge until discrimination is developed. Then he or she discovers that all of this is transient, and sees what is only apparent and superficial and becomes dissatisfied with it. Such knowledge is said to be "neti, neti," not this, not that. Through a process of elimination, the seeker at length comes to what "ought to be known . . . the beginningless supreme Eternal," as Krishna told Arjuna in the Bhagavad Gita (13:12). Brahman, the source of all knowledge, is found.

The most obvious way to stimulate buddhi-manas or the higher mind and intuition is by deep study. Choose a book or article that challenges your understanding, something of importance from the spiritual or metaphysical point of view. Blavatsky's *The Secret Doctrine* is suitable for deep students of Theosophy. Her mystical work, *The Voice of the Silence,* is also appropriate, as is the little work by Krishnamurti as a young boy, *At the Feet of the Master.* You may have your own challenging favorites of metaphysical teachings or of mystical and poetic expressions of the spiritual life.

Pause often in your reading, highlighting provocative ideas. Dwell on obscure passages and difficult ideas. You might cover only a single page in a session, or even a single paragraph. Think deeply over the ideas, trying to grasp them fully and working out how they relate to life.

As a more strictly meditative practice, you could choose a single idea on which to focus, directing all thought toward it. It could be a virtue you hope to cultivate, such as patience or loving-kindness, or an idea like evolution and the growth of the soul. Contemplating abstract metaphysical principles, such as the growth of consciousness through evolution, stimulates the higher mind while it develops concentration. You might choose a short, cryptic passage that inspires you to search for insight. Whatever you decide on, keep your mind focused on it and contemplate its meaning for a time. Besant recommends slowly reading and pondering a short paragraph, so that all your thoughts are absorbed in it (*The Self and Its Sheaths* 95). Then, she says, while keeping the mind concentrated and alert, drop all thoughts for a moment and rest in silence. Besant tells us, "If you want to gain [the sutras'] inner essence, if you want them . . . for the feeding of the Soul within, then . . . in silent meditation, when the senses are quiet and the mind is tranquil, when the light of the SELF is shining, take a sutra and listen to it in its own words alone, and you will learn a spiritual truth that no argument will avail to reach" (*The Self and Its Sheaths* 5).

When the mind is silent, which sometimes occurs after deep concentration, subtle influences from higher levels can emerge into consciousness. As with any form of meditation, this practice must be repeated regularly for it to have a growing and lasting effect.

You can see from Theosophy's teaching of the Self and its powers and principles—our luminous shadows—that there are ranges of experience far beyond our waking everyday awareness. Learning to concentrate and quiet the mind, to become more sensitive through mindfulness, to stretch the mind beyond its ordinary limits through contemplation, you begin to open to unfamiliar areas of your being. As you expand the limits of conscious experience and awaken higher potentials, you are deliberately unfolding in yourself what in time will be unfolded in all humanity. You are working along with the progress of evolution.

The Intuition: Knowledge by Fusion

Every one of us possesses the faculty, the interior sense, known as intuition, . . . the only faculty by means of which men and things are seen in their true colors. It is an instinct of the soul, which grows in us in proportion to the use we make of it . . . . [It] awakens the spiritual senses in us and the power to act.

H. P. Blavatsky

Jean is teaching a handicapped teenager to throw a pot on the potter's wheel. She perceives that he has not grasped the idea of centering. The right words pop into her head as she demonstrates the proper technique and leads the boy to get the idea. She has intuited his problem and found just the right way to get through to him.

A potter, singer, and songwriter, Jean hits upon the "just right" way to express her ideas and emotions through her arts. Her works are original and show independent spirit. She can turn the same intuitive faculty to understanding people and their problems and communicating with them. This gift shows in the way she teaches pottery making and in her relations with her friends, who often come to her for advice and counseling.

Jean operates from intuitive vision rather than from will or planned purpose. When she gets an idea for a piece of sculpture or a song, she is convinced that her vision is valid. Her ideas rarely follow on previous ones but come afresh. She sees a vision of the whole and works out details as she goes along rather than building the whole from the parts. She is ingenious at overcoming difficulties as she proceeds. She does not think through the solutions in a step-by-step way; they come to her holistically.

Jean's mind works quickly. She jumps to conclusions without the gradual process of rational, linear thinking. She grasps significance and meaning immediately. On the Myers-Briggs Type Indicator, she would be classified as intuitive because of her emphasis on wholes and extravert because she is oriented to the outer world. But artistic people are not the only intuitives. Others are found in the business world, especially among CEOs and entrepreneurs; they can also be found as teachers, counselors, research scientists, design engineers, inventors, musicians, social activists, and writers.

Though undervalued in our scientifically oriented culture, intuition is a valid way of knowing. As discussed in chapter 1, C. G. Jung included intuition along with sensation, thinking, and feeling in his classification of ways of functioning. It is a universal human ability. Australian aborigines, who have an uncanny instinct for finding sources of liquid and food in desert areas, access intuition in a state of consciousness called the "Dream Time" (Shallcross and Sisk 46–47). As many psychotherapists including Jung recognize, there is more wisdom in the total organism than in just the conscious mind. Frances Vaughan refers to "an intuitive process that calls for accessing levels of awareness that are not available to habitual ways of thinking" (*The Shadows of the Sacred* 257). In Eastern thought, intuition is considered a faculty that develops during the course of spiritual growth. One aim of Yoga is the systematic cultivation of intuition, which is considered a function of higher levels of consciousness on which a wide range of knowledge is available.

There are many studies of intuition, and there was even a journal called *Intuition*. Businesses are hiring workshop leaders to train managers in developing intuition. In these workshops, you might see vice presidents and CEOs lost in guided fantasies, or giving a right brain (subjective, emotional) report of an accident, or finding metaphors for the way their company works. One manager compared his company to a car with five drivers, all with steering wheels unattached to the car's wheels. Participants are encouraged to pay attention to such images and ideas, even if they seem "off the wall," as they may express a useful insight.

You have intuition. It tells you to do something or not to do it. It pulls you in a certain direction so that you are at the right place at the right time. It tells you that your idea or intention "feels right" or "feels wrong." It shows you new relationships between ideas you've been working with so that all the pieces of the puzzle fit. It comes suddenly and unexpectedly. You feel elated and want to express your insight in words or action.

Examples of Intuitive Insight

Some of the changes in how we think and live have come from intuition. In the nineteenth century, Elias Howe, a first-rate machinist, tried to invent a sewing machine, but he repeatedly failed. The eye for the thread was in the middle of the needle's shaft in his models. One night he had an elaborate dream that was very real to him. He was captured by a fierce tribe and taken to their king, who commanded him to finish the sewing machine at once on pain of death.

He tried but failed. Warriors surrounded him. They were going to execute him with spears. He noticed that near the tips of the spears were eye-shaped holes. He woke up and immediately designed a model sewing machine with the eye for the thread at the tip of the needle, as on the spears and on today's sewing machines.

The psychologist Abraham Maslow refers to two types of scientists (Goldberg 20). One type resembles tiny marine animals, like corals, that build up bit by bit from facts. The other type contains the "eagles of science" who take imaginative flights and produce revolutions of thought. Maslow claimed that Einstein, an eagle, took "intuitive leaps," that his theories were "free inventions of the imagination." His "thought experiments" were visualizations, often done while he shaved. In one of his thought experiments, Einstein imagined twin brothers, one of whom stayed at home on earth, while the other rode around the universe on a beam of light. Einstein saw from this exercise in imagination that the earthling would age faster than the universal traveler. His revolutionary theory of the relativity of time came to him through this fantasy.

In a Sidney Harris cartoon, "The Creative Moment," Einstein is shown at a blackboard, baggy pants and all, writing "$E = ma^2$, $E = mb^2$." The humor of the cartoon is its depiction of Einstein's theory as coming from a logical linear process, whereas Einstein himself said, "The intellect has little to do on the road to discovery. There comes a leap in consciousness, call it intuition or what you will, and the solution comes to you and you don't know how or why."

Helen Keller did not affect the world with her intuition in the same way Einstein did, but it changed her life. Before the age of six this blind and deaf girl was wild and unsocialized, eating with her hands and unable to care for herself in any way. Then Annie Sullivan, a gifted teacher, came to the Keller home to help Helen. She tapped words into Helen's hand in Morse code, but Helen did not associate the taps with meaning. One day Annie took Helen to the pump house, and while she tapped W-A-T-E-R into one hand, she pumped water onto the other hand. Helen had a breakthrough. She got the connection. By the end of the day she had learned thirty words. She also started to become socialized and manageable. Later she wrote, "I understood that what teacher was tapping into my hand meant that cool something. That word 'water' dropped into my mind like the sun in a frozen winter world. It woke me up" (Houston 117).

In a similar way, very young babies learn to connect sounds with objects, to see that a word can stand for something else. We have all had this fundamental intuitive breakthrough. The extent of this basic human ability sets us apart from animals. Language is a hallmark of being human, and it is learned by each child through an intuitive insight.

What Is Intuition?

The Merriam-Webster dictionary defines intuition as "the act or faculty of knowing directly, without the use of rational processes." Additional meanings of the word are "innate or instinctual knowledge" and "a quick and ready apprehension." The word "intuition" comes from the Latin *in* + *tuiri,* "to look (directly) at." Intuition is knowing something from inside rather than outside. Dane Rudhyar, a philosopher and composer, calls it "a mode of supersensible perception, a spiritual 'seeing'"(Shallcross and Sisk 52). It can be like a lightning flash that suddenly illuminates a dark landscape.

Intuition is associated with *buddhi,* a Sanskrit term for the unitive aspect of our nature (see chapter 1). The English word "intuition" is an inadequate translation of that term. Buddhi, a human principle and fundamental aspect of the self, is different from the mind. As action is the function of the physical body, emotion the function of *kama* or the emotions, thinking the function of *manas* or mind, so intuition is a function of buddhi. This principle is part of the deep, interior aspect of consciousness, close to the ground of being—the One Life, God, or Brahman. It is part of the transpersonal Self. Yet intuition, on a lower octave, is also a here-and-now faculty that we can use daily.

Thinking and Intuition

The intuitive way of knowing is fundamentally different from that of the mind. Thinking is representational or deals with abstractions; it is the map rather than the territory. When you think, you create an inner representation of reality through symbols or words, which you manipulate. You consider the object of thought as something "out there," apart from yourself as the thinker. You think *about* something, by means of these interior representations (see chapter 5).

By contrast, intuition deals intimately and directly with realities, not with their symbolic representations. Words cannot convey the essence of a sensory experience, such as the color blue. Yet you instantaneously know what blue is when you see it. This immediate apprehension is also characteristic of intuitive knowledge, by which we know something with our "whole being with total conviction," as Virginia Tower wrote in describing the magical moment of intuitive insight (20):

> That instant of tranquility is like an interval when the
> movement of sea water on a rocky beach pauses and becomes
> lucid just long enough for the eye to catch the panorama of
> glistening shells and sea life upon the floor of the ocean. It is
> a strange and wonderful moment of clarity and conviction.

Thinking and intuition as contrasting modes of knowing have recently been studied in research into the right and left hemispheres of the brain. Experiments were made on patients whose connections between the hemispheres of their brains had been severed during surgery. Those experiments showed that the left side is largely responsible for analysis, logic, language, and views of the world as consisting of discrete, separate things. By contrast, the right side synthesizes and grasps phenomena with unity and fullness. It is holistic and intuitive. These characteristics are typical of buddhi or intuition.

Arthur Deikman, a psychiatrist, distinguishes two modes of consciousness that relate to the left and right brain (30–35). The "instrumental" mode of consciousness automatically perceives boundaries, discriminates between ourselves and others, and sees us as separate from everything else. You are in this mode when you deal with the practicalities of daily life, like shopping, writing checks, composing a business letter, and making a "to do" list. The "receptive" mode of consciousness, on the other hand, relaxes your sense of boundaries and gives you a sense of merging with the environment, as in a hot bath, enjoying a sunset, or meditation. In the receptive mode, your thinking slows down and verbal meanings blur. Your sense of being a distinct self softens. You are no longer controlling things but are open and receptive. Deikman calls this mode the "spiritual self" because in it one is "other-centered" and identified with the larger life process. It is characterized by service rather than gain for oneself. Intuition is more likely to occur in this receptive, right-brain mode.

The intuition, however, does not work in a vacuum. It enlightens the mind; it does not eliminate the mind. The philosopher Immanuel Kant, in his book *Critique of Pure Reason,* held that "thought without intuition is blind, and intuition without thought is empty." Intuition often occurs after the mind has struggled with a problem. The solution for Howe's sewing machine came in a dream after long pondering (as mentioned in chapter 5). Kekule, a Flemish chemist of the nineteenth century, had a famous dream-inspired breakthrough. He spent years wrestling with the structure of the benzene molecule. One evening, exhausted from trying to figure it out, he dozed by the fire. He had a vision of atoms swirling together. After a while, he perceived structures in the mass: the atoms twisted into snake-like shapes. Then one of the snakes grabbed its tail with its mouth. The chemist awoke startled, knowing that benzene atoms are structured in a ring. This insight was soon confirmed, and it laid the groundwork for the modern structural theory of organic chemistry.

By definition, intuition is always right. However, urges from the unconscious can suddenly pop into awareness, imitating intuition. It is not always easy to distinguish a true intuition from such an impulse motivated by desire. An impulse is apt to satisfy wishful thinking and inflate the ego, while intuition is holistic. Impulses usually pass quickly, while an intuition persists and even becomes nagging.

Inspiration

Like Mercury, the Roman messenger of the gods with his winged cap and sandals, intuition brings messages from another realm. The painter Paul Klee said that his hand was entirely the tool of a distant will, and his fellow artist Vasili Kandinski said he had to wait for the dictates of a mysterious voice. Mozart did not think that he produced his compositions; rather, they came to him spontaneously. He explained how thoughts crowded into his mind. "Those which please me I keep in my head and hum them. . . . Once I have my theme, another melody comes, linking itself to the first one, in accordance with the needs of the composition as a whole; the counterpoint, the part of each instrument, and all these melodic fragments at last produce the entire work. Then my soul is on fire with inspiration" (Shallcross and Sisk 50). Plato said of such inspiration or intuition that "truth flashes upon the soul like a flame kindled by a leaping spark."

Intuition and inspiration are apt to come when the conscious, controlling ego is not in focus. Frances Vaughan acknowledges this when she says that the intuition "calls for accessing levels of awareness that are not available to habitual ways of thinking" (*Awakening Intuition* 257). Intuition is invited by a receptive mode, by relaxing and quieting the mind, by a dreamy state, or by actual dreaming. In what is called the "alpha" state, brain waves are slowed down from the alert, waking "beta" state. Some artists invoke their muse by meditation practices. However, intuition can also come in moments of crisis, or simply from deep contemplation.

Buddhi as Intuition

Intuitions, whether or not they originate in buddhi, can impress you at many levels. Lama Govinda says that "intuition may be active on all levels, from the sensuous to the highest spiritual experience" (*Foundations of Tibetan Mysticism* 77). Frances Vaughan also holds that spiritual intuition "is the basic ground from which all other forms of intuition are derived" (*Awakening Intuition* 80). According to this view, intuition can be experienced in various ways and can reflect in or stimulate various principles.

Buddhi in itself is the "unity sense." At the higher reaches of buddhic experience, your consciousness merges with what you perceive. But intuition experienced on lower levels is not necessarily accompanied by a sense of unity, although ordinary intuition does imply some kind of unitive connection with the situation at an inner, unconscious level, as when you somehow know to be at a certain place at just the right time.

Levels of Expression

Intuition can be expressed in physical, emotional, and mental ways. At the physical level, you might experience an intuition as a gut feeling, as a tingling sensation, or even as a pull to the right or the left. If you are intuiting a tough situation ahead, you might get a headache, stomachache, or shoulder tension. Or you might just get up and do something, even though you don't know why, which turns out to be the right thing. For example, one rainy day an accountant parked his car in the usual place at work. Then, for no reason, he got back in the car and moved it. Later that day a large tree was uprooted because of unstable ground due to excessive rain, and it fell where the car was first parked.

If you get an intuition emotionally or through empathy, you may be picking up another person's mood, even though you are not aware of any outward signs of it. Or something you plan "feels right" or "feels wrong." You might have an immediate like or dislike for someone, even love at first sight. However, emotional reactions can come, not from intuition, but from what you hope for or fear. For instance, you might be drawn to a particular car on the dealer's lot, which turns out to be a lemon. It takes discrimination to distinguish personal emotion from intuition.

When you experience intuition mentally you get words, phrases, metaphors, symbols, pictures, numbers, or ideas. These may pertain to concrete things perceived by the lower mind, such as the needle on Howe's sewing machine. Or they may be abstract such as gravity or relativity, perceived by the higher mind. Images are a common expression of the intuition. Jung said that the Self (his term for the transpersonal part of the personality) feeds images to the ego. Images may give you hints to solve practical problems or insight into your internal state and condition. Sometimes you understand the message immediately, and sometimes it needs to be interpreted.

Invoking Images

To invoke and interpret images, Marcia Emery developed a technique called the "Mindshift Method," consisting of six steps (26–32):

1. Define the problem
2. Center
3. Become receptive
4. Elicit imagery
5. Interpret images
6. Apply

To use this technique, first you define the problem clearly and write it down. Then you center yourself by using an affirmation or focusing phrase, such as "Peace, be still" or "I am the Self." Then, you become receptive by using a relaxation technique, such as a few minutes of quiet deep breathing followed by deliberately relaxing your shoulders and other areas of your body. Next, you watch for images, which may come spontaneously or which you may elicit by visualization or fantasy—Emery suggests many such visualizations. Next, you interpret the images, and if you do not see their relevance immediately, you can use a technique such as word associations until you get an "aha!" feeling that you have hit on the right idea. Finally, when you know the solution to your problem, you implement it.

A professor of English went through the steps of this formula in a workshop. She wanted to change jobs and was looking for a sense of direction. The clues that came from her visualization were a pen and a book that fell open to the word "God." She took these to mean that she should do some kind of spiritual writing. She applied for a work-study scholarship and spent some months starting a book on mysticism in English poetry. Afterwards, she relocated, found work teaching, and continued to work on the book. The book was never finished, but she began writing spiritually oriented poetry, some of which was published.

The psychologist Philip Goldberg agrees that intuition can give a sense of direction. He says there is "untapped power and wisdom within us . . . part of ourselves that—although obscured by bad habits and ignorance—understands who we are and what we need and is programmed to move us toward the realization of our highest potential" (16).

Extrasensory Perception

Some authors, such as Frances Vaughan and Marcia Emery, consider extrasensory perception to be an expression of intuition. However, spiritual traditions tend to separate the two, holding that intuition is spiritual whereas supernormal powers like telepathy, precognition, and clairvoyance are mundane. According to the Indian sage Patañjali's *Yoga Sutras* (3:38), the ordinary *siddhis* (supernormal powers) are obstacles that can distract a seeker from the spiritual path. H. P. Blavatsky explains that there are two kinds of siddhis: one kind uses lower psychic and mental energies, while the other is spiritual and demands the highest form of Yoga or spiritual training to develop (*Voice* 73).

In practice, it is often hard to draw a line between extrasensory perception and intuition. Some experiences we may call intuition—a tingling, an impulse, an emotional response of "it fits" or "it doesn't fit," images that pop into our mind—are perhaps really forms of extrasensory perception. Such perceptions are certainly different from the transcendent unitive experience of pure buddhi. But they may be distant reflections of the unlearned knowledge of buddhi, which stimulates lower principles in different ways. All forms of extrasensory perception may be variations of one basic extrasensory factor, as some theorists have proposed. Perhaps the extrasensory factor and spiritual "knowing" of intuition are different levels on a single spectrum of superphysical knowing.

Extrasensory perception does fit a definition of intuition as knowledge gained without rational processes. Physical sensations, which do not rely on rationality, have their counterparts in clairvoyance and clairaudience—seeing or hearing that is not sense-based. Telepathy and precognition often come spontaneously to the mind, without figuring things out. But extrasensory perception usually lacks the overall perspective of intuition. For example, sensing that a prospective boss is not so nice does not necessarily mean that overall the job will not work out well.

Aspects of Buddhi

I. K. Taimni refers to intuition as "the illuminating power behind the mind"(162). He perceives it as something deeper and more spiritual than hunches or extrasensory perception. He also associates more faculties with buddhi than just intuition in the popular sense of the term—namely, intelligence and understanding, contrasted with mental intellect and rote knowledge. Using our mind as an intellectual vacuum cleaner, we can gather up voluminous facts without perceiving their relationship to one another or the significance and application of what we have learned. But when it is energized by buddhi, the higher mind sees the grand design behind the details, like finding a hidden pattern among the random pieces in a child's puzzle.

Another characteristic of buddhi or intuition, according to Taimni, is discrimination. When you distinguish between a damaging rumor and the real facts, between someone's appearance and their character, between an accidental mistake and a deliberate obstacle, you are using the intuitive faculty of discrimination. Such discrimination can sort out what is of value from a mass of irrelevant information. Today, when we are inundated with so much information available in every field, as on the Internet, we particularly need this faculty.

The emotions and the mind tend to exaggerate and to give undue importance to trivialities. Buddhi and intuition give a balanced, overall view that puts things in proper perspective. According to Taimni, "Buddhi sees things directly, truly, wholly and in their true perspective, while intellect sees them indirectly, partially and out of perspective" (157).

Spiritual Perception

The quality of buddhi radiates from an enlightened person. Suppose you take a course in Buddhism at a nearby college. The professor has you memorize the Four Noble Truths, the Noble Eightfold Path, the Three Jewels, the twelve *nidanas,* and the five *skandhas.* But you do not catch the spirit of Buddhism as a living way to wisdom. Now suppose you were lucky enough to study with D. T. Suzuki, an enlightened Zen master as well as a professor. You might not remember all the items in all the lists, but you would taste the goal of spiritual practice, which is enlightenment, and be convinced that some have attained it.

Someone limited to lower learning can become complicated and stress the unimportant. An enlightened person is simple and direct and touches us. As Lao-Tzu observes in the *Tao Teh Ching* (chapter 48):

The man of learning gains day by day.
The man of Tao loses day by day.

Those who have caught a glimpse of enlightenment have soul wisdom, not merely head learning, as H. P. Blavatsky noted in *The Voice of the Silence* (147–48). She warns the aspirant that "even ignorance is better than Head-learning with no Soul Wisdom to illuminate and guide it. . . . [The mind] needs the gentle breezes of Soul-Wisdom to brush away the dust of our illusions."

The highest mode of experiencing intuition is through buddhi in itself, independent of sensations, feelings, thoughts, or extrasensory perceptions. Blavatsky describes such intuition as "that light which never shone on sea or land, that ray of divine intuition, the spark which glimmers latent in the spiritual, never-erring perceptions of man and woman" (*Collected Writings* 8:102). Elsewhere, she calls this ray of intuition "the voice of the silence" and says that the power to hear it means the development of perception that is intuitional and spiritual. It can give us insight into the deepest spiritual truths.

Knowledge by Fusion

Taimni calls spiritual intuition "knowledge by fusion." Henri Bergson characterizes it as the operation "by which one places oneself within an object in order to coincide with what is unique in it and consequently inexpressible" (Pearl 32). Frances Vaughan describes it as "a way of knowing in which the separation of subject and object is transcended. The knower becomes one with the known, and knows from inside, by identification with rather than information about what is known" (*Awakening Intuition* 186).

This pure buddhic knowing from within has two aspects—transpersonal knowledge or wisdom, and impersonal love or compassion. Buddhic wisdom concerns transpersonal truths, such as an appreciation of the interconnection of everything and perception of the organic wholeness behind the world. Thomas Carlyle wrote:

> There is, apart from intellect, in the make-up of every superior identity a wondrous something that realizes, without argument, an intuition of the absolute balance of the whole of this multifarious mad chaos of fraud we call the world: soul-sight of that divine clue and unseen thread which holds the whole congeries of things. (Chari 28)

Walt Whitman achieved this kind of unification. He would lie on the grass just loafing to "invite the soul." Then he would commune with a blade of grass. Through intense communion with this one small living thing, he became one with all being: "Like some mercurial substance the self penetrates into the heart of all being. . . . The intuitive vision rends the veil . . . and penetrates into the core of the object, for all the true nature of the object is in its interiority" (Chari 38).

Sympathy, Empathy, Compassion

Fusion with the object of knowledge evokes various degrees of sympathy, empathy, and compassion. Sympathy is sharing the feelings or interests of another person, such as joy at another's good fortune or sorrow for their pain. Empathy is deeper than that; it is the capacity to know what another experiences, as though from within that being. Jane Goodall, rather than objectively observing the chimps she studied, came to share their feelings and concerns by living among them. In her book *A Feeling for the Organism*, Evelyn Keller describes how Nobel laureate and geneticist Barbara McClintock developed "a feeling for the organism" in which she was able to make discoveries because she felt she "got inside" the corn she was studying (Keller 148–49, 197–207). Influenced by Tibetan Buddhism, McClintock cultivated a meditative state before making her scientific observations.

Compassion has elements of empathy and sympathy but adds to them a desire to help alleviate the suffering of others. We saw compassion on a worldwide scale when television images of starving children in Africa or the horrific events of September 11, 2001, evoked an outpouring of help—by the heroic action of firefighters, by contributions from people everywhere, and by benefit performances of rock stars. Radha Burnier, the international president of the Theosophical Society and a Sanskrit scholar, observes, "Only when the mind has glimpses of unity does it begin to care. Then it cannot rest till it finds the way out of sorrows" (12).

You have no doubt sensed a softening of your own boundaries under certain conditions—when you are absorbed watching the night sky, or the ocean, or a landscape, or a majestic tree, or when you have lost yourself in a moving work of art or compelling music. You may have empathized deeply with another person, perhaps a child, looking through their eyes, perceiving as they perceive, and understanding as they do. It is easy to say what another should do from our own point of view. The rarer experience of understanding the other from within comes from buddhi. A sense of connectedness, compassion, impersonal love, and spontaneous wish to help without any personal motive are pure expressions of buddhi.

In such experiences of merging, we begin to awaken an expansion of love that tends toward universal consciousness. From the viewpoint of Vedantic philosophy, V. K. Chari observes that intuitive identification and mystical abstraction are simultaneous processes: "Even as the self knows itself as the transcendental subject, it expands and becomes all" (108).

Identification with objects of knowledge leads to a wider union with the divine—God, Brahman, or the Christ within—and to the realization that atma is the divine energy that powers the whole cosmic process. Buddhi radiates the ultimate light of oneness, and that light becomes refracted into the seven human powers or principles.

Using Intuition Ethically

According to Theosophical teachings, developing the buddhic principle is humanity's next step in evolution. We have been concentrating on developing our mental powers for a long time. The full flowering of the mind is still in the distant future, so its development will go on for centuries. But alongside mental development, some people even now are unfolding buddhi, and ways to speed the process of its unfoldment are emerging. However, true intuition must not be confused with imprecise or hasty thinking.

Knowledge gained from intuition, like that from the mind or extrasensory perception, can be used for either good or ill. Though it is rooted in buddhi, even genuine intuition can become tainted by personal concerns, for intuition can be used to serve the ego and turned to ends that can be harmful to oneself or others. Its overview of wholeness and balance can be lost in a desire to use it for personal power or ambition. At a lecture at the Naropa Institute in Colorado, Ram Dass said, "Ambition does to intuition what a weevil does to a granary." Though some intuition may concern personal issues, such as choosing a career or using one's money wisely, true intuition has its roots in buddhi and is beneficial overall, not just for oneself, and certainly not harmful to others.

Part of the recent upsurge of interest in intuition is based on a desire to improve profits in business. There is nothing wrong with using intuitive insights to make business decisions, so long as they do not result in unethical practices. But, as observed by Ellen Armstrong (81), "There is the question of how intuition is used. Can it be another noble impulse debased or perverted by becoming a conscienceless servant to the gods of profit and power?" It is important to look for the overall consequences of acting on what seems like intuition and to be sure that the outcome will be fair and ethical. In addition, genuine intuition is not limited to worldly interests but gives insight into spiritual matters.

Cultivating Intuition

You can cultivate intuition and learn to hear its "still, small voice," but whether or not you achieve that goal depends on time, place, mood, attitude, and state of mind. If you are depressed or fatigued, intuition may be blocked. For true intuition to appear, you need to rise above strong desires or fears. If you are overly busy or your time is too structured, intuition may not be able to impress your mind, for an overactive mind with no time to cultivate stillness is not receptive to subtle impressions. If you are not open to something new and are afraid to take risks, you are not likely to let intuition in. If you don't believe that you have the potential for developing intuition, you probably won't. It grows in those who encourage it.

There are many methods to develop and enhance intuition. One such exercise, said to have been developed by Sigmund Freud, is the following (Emery 107): You have to make a yes-no decision, such as whether to suggest to your boss an innovation in the procedure of another department. The suggestion could be risky, because the department is not your concern. Should you do it? You flip a coin: heads yes, tails no. But how do you feel about the decision made by the coin? Relieved? Frustrated? Anxious? At peace? Noting your feelings, you reconsider and make the decision on the basis of your reaction to the coin flip, not on the flip itself. You already knew unconsciously what to do. The coin flip only brought the knowledge to your conscious mind.

Helena Blavatsky also taught a simple but difficult method for awakening intuition (*Collected Writings* 12:499). Though she was eager to teach, when her students came to her with questions, she told them to think deeply about the matter in all its aspects and find an answer for themselves. Her recommendation encourages independent thinking and also stimulates the intuition.

Marcia Emery's Mindshift Method, cited above, similarly helps to develop intuition, as do various techniques in the books of Frances Vaughan and Philip Goldberg. Keeping a journal to record your intuitive impressions encourages more intuitive impressions to come. Note whether your impressions proved to be valid. As you look over this record from time to time, you become sensitive to the difference between experiencing true intuition and passing impulses.

Communing with nature also helps quiet the mind and permits the play of buddhi upon it. As Virginia Tower poetically informs us, we get glimmerings through "those quiet promptings that come to us in the dead of night or in some isolated moment of acute perception inspired by the sight of a tree, a cloud, a waterfall. Instead of putting that moment regretfully aside, we encourage its meaning—as one blows on a tiny ember in order to bring a flame into being" (49–50).

Another way to evoke buddhi is to ponder and digest important parts of what you read, as explained in chapter 5. Try to penetrate to the core of the meaning beyond the words. Verses of poetry or challenging spiritual works are good for such contemplation. The mystic work *Light on the Path* has many suitable passages, such as this:

> Listen to the song of life. . . . Life itself has speech and is never silent. And its utterance is not, as you that are deaf may suppose, a cry: it is a song. Learn from it that you are part of the harmony; learn from it to obey the laws of the harmony. (Collins 24–25)

Contemplating this passage may show you the universe, not as a mechanical process or system, but in its dynamic wholeness as a song, full of harmony and joy.

A Christian variation of intuitive reading is called *lectio divina,* or "divine reading." One version is as follows: Take some time to breathe deeply and center yourself. Then read a passage, such as an inspired bit of Scripture, over and over slowly until a phrase stands out. Then close your eyes and repeat the phrase until you have an intuitive response—an image, emotional reaction, or insight. Note the response, and then remain quiet for a time. When you feel closure, give thanks for the insight you have received.

Objectively watching your mind without judging it is another entry into buddhic consciousness. If you can observe the mind creating its picture book by imposing its patterns, prejudices, and preconceptions onto reality, you become aware that you are not that mind. You are something deeper that can stand behind and observe your mental process. This insight can open you so that you touch buddhic awareness.

Emptying the mind and dropping preconceptions and expectations is another way to invite buddhi. Blavatsky taught that higher truth cannot be absorbed by a mind filled with preconceptions, prejudice, or suspicion (*Collected Writings* 10:128). In a newspaper article (*Pittsburgh Post-Gazette*, Dec. 22, 1997), Mrs. Norman Vincent Peale confides,

> If I have a problem and I want to get God's guidance, the first thing I do is empty my mind. Then when your mind is empty you're ready to completely relax, and you say:
> Dear God, give me a direction. Tell me what I should do.
> It's amazing how many times you'll get an answer that you didn't think of yourself. As you analyze the idea and start following it, new things will come.

Mrs. Peale's practice is very like Marcia Emery's Mindshift Method, already cited several times: define the problem, center and become receptive, look for a clue such as an image, interpret it, and put it into action. This process can also be applied for spiritual insight.

I. K. Taimni holds that one of the best ways to invoke buddhic consciousness is through devotion, since buddhi can feed directly into the emotions (151). In intense devotion to Jesus, the Buddha, God, or a saint, we lose ourselves in higher consciousness. Taimni especially recommended the *Gayatri*, a Hindu prayer to God as Solar Logos, a powerful center of universal life in our solar system. Repeating a phrase in a state of deep devotion can propel one into buddhic union with the object of devotion. The ancient Jesus prayer ("Lord Jesus Christ, Son of God, have mercy upon me") or a simple statement like "Jesus, I trust in thee" can unite one with Christ consciousness. Psalm 42.1, "As the deer longs for running water, so my soul longs for you, O God," can have a similar effect.

The Buddha taught a meditation that does not require a religious orientation. He said to let the mind "pervade one quarter of the world with thoughts of pity, with thoughts of sympathy and equanimity, and so the second quarter, and so the third, and so the fourth. And thus the whole wide world, above, below, around, and everywhere, he continues to pervade with heart of pity, heart of sympathy, and heart of equanimity, far-reaching, grown great and beyond measure, all embracing" (Goddard 71). The expansion of consciousness evoked by such a meditation helps to break the confines of the individual principles. In such a state, love and compassion flood one's consciousness.

Quieting your mind by the regular practice of meditation opens a track through which insight can reach your conscious mind. It is good to start learning to meditate with a group or else to read a good book on meditation. There are many ways to get started. Some are discussed in chapter 5, such as being aware of your breath without interfering with it, visualizing a meaningful symbol such as the Cross or an image of the Christ or the Buddha, a beautiful scene or natural object, such as a rose, or just white light. Reciting a mantra quiets and focuses the mind, as does reciting or chanting a prayer or affirmation.

When your mind has settled into quiet, rest a while in the stillness. Buddhi can play on a quiet mind and give insight. Even if you do not seek guidance on a specific problem at the moment, a passageway to intuition opens so that insights may come at another time.

Once you establish an opening for it, intuitive awareness can become a familiar state. In its worldly applications, it can help you to make good decisions in everyday life. In its highest reaches, it can lead you to buddhi and the perception of essential unity with all beings. The ancient verses on which Blavatsky's masterwork, *The Secret Doctrine*, is based state that humanity has been given "a mind to embrace the universe" (2:17). Intuition can bring us closer to that transpersonal mind, to "the intuitive experience of the infinity and the all-embracing oneness of all that is" (Govinda, *Foundations* 77).

Chapter 7

The Spiritual Will:
The Transcendent
Principle

Spiritual will is the transcendent principle within us which forms as it were the very heart and core of our being.

I. K. Taimni

Eileen, a shy eighteen-year-old, sits rapt as she listens to the lecture. She has come to the new headquarters building of the Theosophical Society in America in Wheaton, Illinois. She is sitting before the re-nowned Annie Besant, international president of the Theosophical Society, who is visiting the United States. Not even five feet tall, the great orator appears as a towering figure on the platform. Eileen hears her passionate oration about her vision of the Society's spiritual mis-sion, of its potential to uplift and spiritualize a materialistic era. Dr. Besant is appealing to the American Theosophists to join her in her crusade to help the world. Eileen hears her say, "Who will come? Who will help me?" Silently, Eileen vows, "I will!" And she did. From that day till she died in her nineties, Eileen was devoted to Theosophy and helped the cause in any way she could. She became known for "chalk talks" in which her charming drawings illustrated Theosophical ideas.

Annie Besant inspired people like that. She had a way of getting things done by motivating people to help. Before her years in the Theosophical Society, she had been a social activist in turn-of-the-century England. She spearheaded a landmark strike by the "match girls," who worked under deplorable conditions in match manufacturing plants, and helped them win better conditions. She was active in such causes as the abolition of child labor, penal reform, meals for indigent school children, and equal rights for women. She was associated with Charles Bradlaugh in an activist group of Freethinkers and later with George Bernard Shaw in the Fabian Society, a group dedicated to social reform. She and Bradlaugh were taken to court for distributing a pamphlet on birth control, and Besant, a divorcee, lost custody of her children as consequence. She was self-sacrificing and passionate about causes and a fearless warrior in fighting for them.

In later years, while she was president of the Theosophical Society and living in India, Besant agitated for home rule for India. She was imprisoned under house arrest for three months for these activities. After her release, she campaigned even more vigorously and was elected as president of the Indian National Congress, the first woman and only non-Indian to be so honored. She continued to work for the uplift of India through reviving a Hinduism free of superstition, improving education, preserving ancient Indian art, and working to abolish wrongful social customs such as child marriage and the caste system. She devoted herself to regenerating morality and spirituality, to restoring the pride of Indians in their heritage, and to inspiring the respect of others for Indian culture.

This tiny woman was a major force in bold new social movements. A gifted organizer, she could initiate something new and pass it on to others to carry forward. She did not rule with an iron hand, manipulate others, or impose rigid control, as we might think a strong-willed person would do. She was caring and kind and greatly loved, so much so that many Indians called her "Mother" *(amma)*. She led by inspiring others with an ideal and serving as a role model. She was able to overcome obstacles and knew how to bring a plan into actuality. She showed quiet resolve and perseverance and was one-pointed in living by her ideals; her life had long-range direction and commitment. She showed spiritual will.

Will, Volition, Intention

The word *will* is used in so many ways that it may not appear to be a single human capacity. *Webster's New Collegiate Dictionary* gives such synonyms as *desire, wish; disposition, inclination; appetite, passion; choice, determination;* and *request, command.* However, definitions for two of its synonyms, *volition* and *intention*, have common features that suggest the meaning of the term *will* as used here.

Volition is the act of making a choice or decision or the power of choosing or determining. *Intention* is the resolve or determination to act in a certain way. One definition of *will* is a disposition to act according to certain principles or ends, and another is the power of control over one's own actions or emotions.

A picture emerges from these definitions of a human capacity to control things and oneself, to show determined action, to make intentions really happen, and to overcome obstacles. This requires decision making and choice, and choice involves desire or wish. Persons with developed will have a disposition toward chosen, predetermined ends so that their conflicting desires become harmonized and integrated and their energies concentrated on chosen goals. This requires self-control. Like Annie Besant, and even Eileen who formulated a lifelong purpose while listening to Annie Besant, such persons have long-term purpose and commitment.

Free Will?

Will is not one of the types in the Myers-Briggs Type Inventory. Willpower has not been in fashion since the time of Freud, who held that free will is an illusion. Our decisions seem to us to come from our own volition, but Freud uncovered many irrational factors that affect the decisions we make and the actions we take.

Think of a decision you made, such as getting your car fixed, undertaking a new project at work, spending more time with your family, or meditating everyday. You used your rational mind and thought about all the reasons for your decision, maybe even listing pros and cons, but your feelings no doubt also played a part. In addition, you were probably influenced by semiconscious or unconscious memories or desires. Perhaps a similar decision made you feel good some time in the past. Or you had a vague feeling of guilt, that you *should* decide that way, though you are not sure why. Or you unconsciously sensed fulfillment of some long-buried hope. Or your choice might have touched off a forgotten spiritual aspiration. In addition to rational, conscious thought, unconscious and semiconscious feelings, attitudes, and memories are factors in making decisions and in what we do.

Freud said that we are victims of forces of which we are unaware. He found that in psychoanalysis his patients unearthed unconscious urges and forbidden desires, fears, and instinctual forces that are not ordinarily accessible by the conscious mind; we are "lived by the unconscious." Many psychologists and philosophers think it is no longer feasible to posit a special part of the personality, the will or volition, as the seat of choice. Too many other parts of the personality are involved in the choices we make. In contemporary psychological textbooks, *will* is seldom found as a category. Instead you find terms like *purposive behavior, intentionality, decision making, choice,* and *self-control.* But transpersonal psychologist Frances Vaughan refers to "personal power," the ability to choose and carry out intentions, which she admits implies the existence of free will (*Shadows* 154). Other contemporary transpersonal psychologists also concur that we have free will.

Moreover, religious traditions generally consider that humans do have free will to do good or ill, which is one of the hallmarks of being human. St. Augustine held that "God endows us with free will but we can fail to do good." Many theologians consider the human will to be comparable to God's will, which created the world. Theosophy and the esoteric tradition consider will in its highest aspect to be the core of our nature, for spiritual will is an expression of our most essential self, atma.

Aspects of Will: Skillful Will

We are apt to identify will with strong will. When we think of people with will, we might think of take-charge people who are aggressive, forceful, overly self-confident, perhaps forbidding and stern. They may demand their own way and be pushy and bossy, manipulative, and stubborn. They may even be egotistic, ruthless, and hard. But such people have strong personal wills, not spiritual wills.

Annie Besant used spiritual will to achieve purposes without force or coercion, and C. W. Leadbeater called spiritual will the quietest thing in the world. A person with such will is not at the mercy of circumstances but shows determined action, initiative, courage, and daring, but not confrontational force. An integrated person can show the effectiveness and fire of strong will without the negative aspects of an overbearing personal will.

Will is not limited to displays of strength, but has other aspects. Roberto Assagioli in his book *The Act of Will* discusses the "skillful will," the "good will," and the "transpersonal will."

"Skillful will" uses the most effective strategy to make things happen, not necessarily by confrontation. A person with skillful will understands how ideas, emotions, and the body interact and knows how to work with them. Such a person of skillful will does not fight a dark mood but encourages the emotions into a better state through visualization or music or an enjoyable activity. A good leader motivates workers through appealing to their emotions and values rather than through threats or coercion.

The Buddha used skillful will when a woman brought her dead baby to him, asking that he bring the child back to life. The Buddha asked her first to bring him a mustard seed from a house that had not known death. She knocked on many doors and could not find a single house where no one had died. She came back to the Buddha in a different frame of mind, realizing that death is part of life for everyone and accepting her own child's death in this realization. She buried her child and became a disciple of the Buddha.

Larry Dossey cites biofeedback as an example of what he calls "passive will," which is a form of skillful will. Suppose you have high blood pressure and have been referred for biofeedback training to lower it. You certainly cannot bring your blood pressure down through force of will. You are apt rather to raise it that way. In biofeedback training, you are hooked to a device that measures the volume of blood in a finger. You are instructed to make your hands warm. You don't know how to do this, but you try hard to will the warmth a few times and fail. Then somehow you get the sense that you must relax and let go. In a relaxed state you hit on an image, such as dowsing your hands in hot water, that really makes them feel warmer, and they do warm up. By doing this you dilate constricted blood vessels, which lowers your blood pressure. Using passive volition, Assagioli's skillful will, you achieve your purpose.

Aspects of Will: Good Will

Assagioli points out that, like all our powers, will can be used for good or ill. If you work for personal power and wealth, you may achieve them. But, as Joseph Campbell said, when you get to the top of the ladder, you may find that it is leaning against the wrong wall.

Blavatsky, like all ethical teachers, warns against egoistic volition, using willpower for selfish, personal ends that can injure others. In her colorful language, she says, "This is black magic, abomination, and spiritual sorcery" (*Key to Theosophy* 68). To avoid this "abomination," instead of wanting and willing unconsciously, we need to learn to be aware of our motivation so we can know when it is wholly personal and perhaps selfish. Wanting things for ourselves is all right as long as it does not harm others. A good touchstone is to see whether what we want is good, not just for ourselves, but for the whole.

Rollo May, one of the first modern psychologists to respect the will as a legitimate function, points out that our will needs to be balanced with love. A person of strong will typically is less developed in love, and vice versa. Love unites while will can be separative and domineering. Will lacks heart, but love can be weak and sentimental. Love and will need to be integrated and blended to produce the good will (Assagioli, *Act of Will* 195–96). Besant with her ideal of social reform is a prime example of good will with aims that benefit the welfare of others.

Aspects of Will: Transpersonal Will

True mastery in life comes from the level of the transpersonal will, of which the personal will is only a reflection. This higher will of the self has the capacity to direct and harmonize body, emotions, mind, and other lesser functions. By exercising it, one becomes a harmonious whole, so that conflicts are eliminated through single-minded action. An example is the action of teenage boys who tackled a crazed fellow student who had just fired an automatic weapon into a crowded lunchroom. The boys reported that they were not afraid and did not feel heroic but just spontaneously did what was necessary.

You may remember a moment, perhaps in a crisis, when you did not consider yourself or your needs, or even your safety, but were centered wholly on what needed to be done. What Assagioli calls the transpersonal will took over. At such moments when you are wholly integrated within and focused on an action, what you want for yourself turns out to be good for everyone else as well. The spiritual will integrates all the lesser parts of the self into a harmonious whole, so that conflicts are eliminated. In such single-minded action, as Ken Wilber says, "The will is an act of a person's total being" (*Spectrum* 117).

A critical situation can actualize the transpersonal will and change a person. In her book *Kitchen Table Wisdom*, the physician Rachel Naomi Remen tells the story of a woman whose husband was diagnosed with incurable cancer. This woman was so shy that it was painful for her to go to the supermarket or even answer the phone. She depended on her husband to handle contacts with people outside the family. She and her husband were in business together, and he wondered how she would be able to take over the business and support the children financially and emotionally after his death. As his illness progressed, she took on the task of phoning specialists all over the country about it. She assumed more and more business responsibilities, and she was also able to comfort her children. Remen saw this woman a few years later, after the husband's death. She was a different person from the one with crippling shyness whom Remen had known. She was strong and decisive and had made a life of her own. Her desire to help her husband in his illness and her family had given her the impetus to transform shyness and fear into courage by drawing on the spiritual will, the higher potential within.

Assagioli refers to an ongoing process of integration as "psychosynthesis." Through disidentification with the temporary contents of consciousness that pass through our awareness, we come to realize that they are not the true self—that we are not our thoughts, emotions, sensations, roles, opinions, convictions, or attachments, any of which can control us: "We are dominated by everything with which our self becomes identified. We can dominate, direct, and utilize everything from which we disidentify ourselves" (*Act of Will* 211). When we achieve disidentification we are no longer pulled by fragments of ourselves but can exert our will wholly in one direction without their interference.

Here is an exercise in disidentification of the type Assagioli recommended. Make a list of eight or ten roles or social behavior patterns that you play in life: wife or husband, parent, professional person, boss or employee, Christian or Jew or Buddhist or Muslim, spiritual seeker, skier, writer, American, global citizen, and so on. Then choose the four or five most important roles from the list. Of those four or five, choose the one with which you identify the most. Next imagine yourself without having that role. How would it feel? Do you seem diminished? Then eliminate another role, and then another, until you have done away with all the roles on your short list. What is left? Do you still exist as a person? You have gone through many role changes already since childhood. What survived those changes and preserved your sense of being the same person? Practices like this can help us wriggle free from the many externals that we think we are and edge up to what we truly are.

Attention

In addition to the various aspects of will—strong, skillful, good, and transpersonal—the will has several functions. One of these is attention. William James, called the father of modern psychology, in the early years of the century held that attention is essential to the phe-nomenon of will. He gave the example of getting out of bed on a cold morning. You think of the comfort and warmth of the bed. Then you think of what you have to do that day and the conse-quences if you do not do it. You conclude that you must attend to your tasks. Then your will takes over and you are up. James believed that in decision making we are aware of conflicting desires. We weigh them and decide to ignore all but one, then we act on that one. So for James, attention is the key to will.

If you watch your thoughts drifting through your mind for a while, you will see that your attention wanders. You decide to read a book and stay with the story for a while. Then something in it reminds you of the time when you were bird watching and you remember searching for a trumpeter swan, in spite of the cold mists and rain. That makes you feel chilly, so you make a cup of tea. The tea reminds you that you need to go grocery shopping, so you make a list. Then you remember the book and go back to it. Your drifting attention has triggered several actions.

Sometimes your attention is concentrated effortlessly if you are thinking of something that especially interests you. But you may be dismayed to discover that much of the time your mind drifts and is not under your control. However, through intent you can deliber-ately force the mind to stick to one thing in concentrated attention. If you have to study for an examination, you can willfully focus your attention on the chapters you need to absorb. In learning to medi-tate, you get better at keeping your attention from wandering. You start watching your breath or contemplating a sacred image or a seed thought. But soon you are lost in planning refreshments for the discussion group that evening. You dutifully bring your attention back to the object of meditation, only to have it drift off into a memory of a recent conversation. After persistently practicing for some weeks or months, you reach a point where you seldom get lost in passing thoughts, though your mind may still wander to some degree. You have used your will to train your wandering mind.

Intention

In deliberately concentrating, you use intentionality, another characteristic of will. As an experiment, notice your mind as you raise your arm above your head. Can you say how a mental event like deciding to move your arm—an intention—caused physical movement? It is a mystery philosophers have grappled with since the time of Descartes and before. Yet we experience our consciousness controlling our actions countless times every day. We cannot directly affect our autonomic functions like digestion and heartbeat through intention, except perhaps by biofeedback or other special training. But we continuously give orders to our central nervous system with its control of our muscles.

Athletes have developed this ability to an amazing degree. For instance, the driver on a luge, a very fast sled, cannot see the track ahead very well because you have to lie down when you ride on a luge. But you feel every bump. With silent, nonverbal intention, subtle movements of the driver's shoulders and legs steer the luge down a slope, sometimes at ninety miles an hour. Intention does not do the steering, but it gives directions to the muscles that steer.

When we intend something, we often imagine a future event, such as planning a trip or visualizing a golf swing, before performing it. Intention makes it possible for us to make a promise, to plan for the future, to strategize. It is different from a wish, in which we want something but do not do anything to bring it about. Yet it takes more than intention to bring the plan into being; as the old saying goes, "The road to hell is paved with good intentions." Follow-through in getting things done is needed. Will is the power that drives the machinery, whether to pay the bills, cook dinner, write a paper, drive a luge, or tread the spiritual path. Will has been called the power aspect of consciousness.

Will and the Physical World

The relationship between the will and the physical world can be seen in an image of a three-story building reflected in a lake. The upper story of the building, representing atma or will, appears in the lowest level of the reflection in the lake, which symbolizes the physical world. Will is reflected in the physical body. Buddhi or intuition is reflected in kama or the emotions; and higher manas, the philosophical mental level, is reflected in the concrete level of the mind. Thus will resonates in action; intuition resonates in emotions; and higher mind resonates in lower mind.

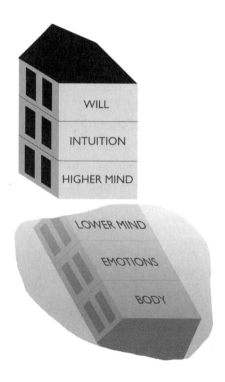

FIGURE 2

This analogy indicates the close relationship between the will and the physical consequences of an intention. You decide to drive to the grocery store. Your muscles follow your direction, take you to the car, drive it under your direction. Your intention is carried out through the will and its connection with physical consequences. The physical world especially embodies the life of atma. Humans are complete only while incarnated in physical existence.

Will and Desire

Blavatsky describes the creative power of the will in what she calls "will-prayer," which is "rather an internal command than a petition." This kind of prayer is not addressed to an external deity but to the "inner man," the transpersonal self. Will-prayer is "an occult process by which finite and conditioned thoughts and desires are translated into spiritual wills and the will." It seems that the energies of desire can be transmuted to both higher spiritual levels and to lower octaves, thereby affecting the external world, for will-prayer "becomes the active or creative force, producing effects according to our desire (*Key* 67–68)."

Freud held that wish, not will, moves us. According to Rollo May, wish and will complement one another. Wish gives warmth and freshness to will, while will gives direction and maturity to wish. Will without wish can yield a stern, repressive Victorian will, while wish alone is driven, infantile, and unfree.

Desire, however, is so potent that it is often mistaken for will. But will has an element of intentionality and is more stable than desire. What we ordinarily call "will" may be only one desire in opposition to another desire. You want to lose weight, but you want to eat rich foods. Your gastronomic desire clashes with your desire to look good and be slim. Blavatsky said that through growth we replace wish or desire by will: "Most men live in and by desire, mistaking it for will. But he who would achieve [spiritually] must separate will from desire, and make his will the ruler; for desire is unstable and ever changing, while will is steady and constant. . . . Will creates intelligently—desire blindly and unconsciously" (*Collected Writings* 8:109).

Blavatsky's remarks about will-prayer and desire versus will give a hint about how to "manifest" what we want by willing it internally, whether finding a parking place, attracting a suitable mate, or discovering appropriate avenues for service. This kind of willing can work. But we can thus "manifest" something that in the long run is a burden and a hindrance to our real aims in life. We need an overall transpersonal perspective toward the good before willing wishes into physical reality.

Levels of Willing

Roberto Assagioli identifies three levels of willing: personal, transpersonal, and a realm where the individual will merges with the universal will. The personal will is centered in ourselves as seemingly separate beings. The transpersonal will operates at the level of the soul or individuality from an impersonal long-range perspective, not just for short-sighted personal gain. In the highest form of will, the personality and even the transpersonal self are inspired by the universal will, call it God or atma, for the good of the whole.

The personal will is bound up with the I-sense. The "I" is necessary for willing at this level because it is an active agent choosing or willing something into being. Writing a letter and taking it to the mailbox does not occur just on its own; "I" cause the action by willing it. An act that occurs by itself, such as blinking an eye, is not willed; "I" did not will it. Rollo May says that the possibility for action that I can perform constitutes will and that I experience myself as a person through my intentionality and will: "The 'I' is the 'I' of 'I can.' . . . I and will are correlated terms" (*Love and Will* 243).

Assagioli concurs. He places the will along with the self or I-sense at the center of his scheme of psychological functions. He seems, however, to be referring to the transpersonal will when he states, "Through the will the I acts on the other psychological functions regulating and directing them" (*Act of Will* 12–13). The personal will has only limited control and regulation of the other functions. You cannot stop an annoying tune from running through the mind or a quiver of anxiety from returning when you think about your new business venture, or your shoulders from tensing when you work on your income tax.

The vehicles each of our principles uses has a life of its own and has its own agenda, which may not be the same as what the "I" and our inmost volition want. For example, your emotions may want to flare up in anger, while at deeper levels you want to be loving and kind. The spiritual guidebook *At the Feet of the Master* (Krishnamurti 9) tells us: "Do not mistake your bodies for yourself—neither the physical body, nor the astral, nor the mental. Each one of them will pretend to be the Self, in order to gain what it wants. But you must know them all, and know yourself as their master"; that is, bring them under the control of your will.

Automatic Responses

As we have seen, in addition to having their own wants, the body, mind, and emotions are bound by habits and conditioning—responses from the past that we automatically act on. Going to the parking lot alone at night, you see an ill-dressed young man in the distance. You hurry to your car and quickly lock the door. A woman with broken English waits on you at the hardware store. You tense up, expecting her not to know the stock or to be of any help. Your boss frowns,

you gird yourself for a reprimand. We are at the mercy of numberless little conditioned responses that cause us to act and think in
ways that are automatic and not considered. We can begin to overcome these by becoming aware of them and willfully choosing
whether or not to act on them.

We are multivolitional, driven by many wills. But our lives
can be effective only when we are not controlled by the lesser urges
at peripheral levels of our consciousness. Ken Wilber expresses the
Theosophical view when he says that the will is a higher-order unity
that is above and prior to all other functions (*Sex, Ecology, Spirituality* 46). As Annie Besant points out, the will is free only when
we, as the self, have mastered our various principles (*Study in Consciousness* 269). Lesser volitions and desires become subordinated to
a stronger intention; the many wills tend to become a single overar-
ching will. We can begin to overcome the lesser conflicting desires
and habits by becoming aware of them and willfully choosing to
override them.

Volition can be cultivated; we can develop willpower. William
James suggested doing useless exercises to train the will. For instance,
try standing on a chair for ten minutes everyday, or listen to a clock
tick and make a certain gesture on every fifth tick, or get up ten or
fifteen minutes earlier than usual. Such practices will no doubt help
you to master your various vehicles, but you can achieve the same
purpose with activities that you find more useful.

Try training your emotions by being patient when someone
annoying is making demands on you, or put a limit on how much
television you watch, or make choices not based on personal prefer-
ence, such as choosing foods that are good for you rather than your
favorites. The practice of mindfulness, simply paying full attention
to whatever you are doing without the mind wandering, is perhaps
the most powerful way to train the will. It is hard to do at first

because our overactive minds tend to run on most of the time. But with practice it gets easier and brings a kind of peace to daily life.

Metaneeds and B-Values

The transpersonal will is not concerned with details of personal life but with larger issues, such as long-range purpose, direction, and meaning. Abraham Maslow, a pioneer in humanistic and transpersonal psychology, in his *Motivation and Personality* describes a hierarchy of needs that we all have. In addition to physiological needs such as for food, we have psychological needs for safety, for belonging and love, and for esteem. We also have higher needs: to know and understand, to appreciate and express beauty, to actualize our potentiality fully in a healthy, nonneurotic way. Maslow found that higher needs emerge only when lower needs are met.

Maslow studied certain self-actualizing people who had passed out of the normal range of the hierarchy of needs (*The Farther Reaches of Human Nature* 126–148). Their values, at least to some extent, were not based on lack or deficiency (D-values) but were "being values" (B-values) that emerge only when normal needs are largely filled. These subjects were motivated by "metaneeds" that include an inner drive toward finding an overview of one's place in life and in the cosmos—a drive toward a deep transpersonal realization of the purpose of life. Metaneeds are involved with B-values, such as transcendence of self, unitive consciousness, mystical experience, bliss, awe, sacralization of everyday life, and cosmic awareness. This level of transpersonal need is usually latent, but in some people, even if they are not fully self-actualized, it emerges and demands satisfaction.

Leo Tolstoy, the Russian novelist, philosopher, and mystic, wrote in his autobiographical work *A Confession* about a gnawing emptiness he experienced during a certain period in his life. Not yet fifty years of age, he had what he considered "complete good fortune," a good wife who loved him, good children, wealth, a large estate, and vigorous physical health. His name was famous. There was nothing that he wanted for himself. Yet he was miserable. He went through his usual activities, but "there was no life, for there were no hidden wishes the fulfillment of which I would consider reasonable." Even when considering plans for his children's educa- tion or ways for the peasants on his land to prosper, he would ask himself, "What does it matter?" He described his inner state: "The power that drew me away from life was stronger, fuller, more wide- spread than any mere wish. It was a force similar to the former striv- ing to live, only in a contrary direction. All my strength drew me away from life" (Assagioli, *Act of Will* 107–109). In Maslow's terms, Tolstoy had a "metaneed." Assagioli calls despair like Tolstoy's the "central drama for humans," because we are unable to find peace without finding meaning.

Gautama Buddha is an example of one who lived for B-values and was motivated by metaneeds. He was not concerned with the needs of his personality but with finding meaning and helping oth- ers to find it, to which he devoted his life. The legend of Gautama portrays him as a prince who had every possible luxury, completely shielded from any kind of pain or sadness. One day, against his father's wishes, he went out into the world. There he encountered someone who was desperately sick, someone who was old and weak, and someone who was dying. He was mystified by those encounters and consequently resolved to find the cause of pain and sorrow. One night he left his home, wife, and child and became a mendicant monk living in the forest.

For many years Gautama meditated with wise men, trying a variety of spiritual practices and becoming emaciated from extreme austerities. Although he had not found the understanding of life he sought, he persisted in the search. Finally, he sat down under a fig tree and vowed that he would not rise until he had found the answer to sorrow and suffering. As a result of that intention, he achieved enlightenment: he perceived the workings of the human mind and the way it produces suffering, and he found peace. For the next forty years, he wandered around India teaching the Four Noble Truths and the Noble Eightfold Path that leads to the end of suffering and to peace. The Buddha is usually thought of as the ideal example of compassion, but he also illustrates indomitable will because he persisted in his search and his commitment to help others.

The Calling

There is an inner direction and meaning that inheres at the transpersonal level in every life. We are at least partly conscious of this as a calling or "vocation." In a sense, vocation is "to hear a voice." Jung said, "Who has vocation hears the voice of the inner man; he is *called*" (Assagioli, *Act of Will* 115). The call comes from the spiritual will that pulls or pushes in a certain direction so that one feels inner inclinations over a long period of time.

Certain themes emerge during one's life, perhaps expressed as a full-time career, perhaps as humble activities concerned with small, everyday acts and attitudes. You may not be an artist or poet, but simply find joy in looking at art, reading beautiful literature, creating beauty in your garden, or collecting beautiful things. You may not be a doctor or nurse, but promote healing by listening to friends' problems, cheering someone who is depressed, shopping for your elderly neighbor, or authorizing leave for an employee with serious family problems. You may not negotiate between great factions, but simply build bridges between people in conflict with one another in your family, in the workplace, or in your social life. You may not be a spiritual teacher, but simply show others what is real and true, not fanciful and imagined, in everyday situations. If you are fulfilling your higher calling, whether in large or small ways, you are expressing the transpersonal will. Taimni says that "the spiritual will is the source of that eternal, dynamic urge drawing us toward our destined goal of perfection" (179).

The various parts we play in the order of things emerge as we blend our personality more and more with the transpersonal self. This means disidentifying with routine, habitual ways of being and clearing the way for the self's guidance in decisions and in our way of life. It means inviting the spiritual will by standing by what is authentic for us, what we deeply want, what gives us the sense of fulfilling ourselves and our destiny. Virginia Tower suggests an exercise that can help to open the mind to the thrust of purpose from within:

> At times when you are very quiet and when desire and emotion have become stilled, you can observe the quiet shaping of yourself from within—can see the form you are intended to take, the work you should do—your function in the environment and the scheme of things. It is very important to see this. This is not forecasting as the astrologers and soothsayers do it; it is a deep and intelligent observation of your own nature and propensities. When you have seen yourself clearly, then it stops all the speculation and striving, all the doubt and uncertainty. It puts an end to ambition. In the rarefied atmosphere of truth, your words, your thoughts, your acts will bring manifest form to that quiet vision. (83)

The vision of one's essential purpose comes from the spiritual will and the transpersonal Self. Assagioli speaks of "the will's central position in man's personality and its intimate connection with the core of his being, his very self" (*Act of Will* 6). The will has its source in atma, which is the source of all power and enlivens our entire being.

Atma is not far off in some distant heaven; it energizes us at every level all the time. It is that central core that integrates our principles into a whole. Without it, we would be like sleepwalkers or Alzheimer patients without control of our minds and emotions. The different aspects of ourselves would operate on their own without central, overall direction. But if all of our principles are energized and integrated by the spiritual will so that our many powers are harmonized and we act as a whole being, we totally express spiritual will in all that we do.

Transcendent Will

Atma, or universal consciousness, is the source of awareness in us and in all life. If we could strip away all the contents of our consciousness—all the thoughts, feelings, and sensations—and come face to face with bare consciousness itself, we would experience pure atma, our essential self. We would discover that awareness does not stop at our skin; it is not really "our" awareness but is boundless and permeates all life.

Some Western philosophers and mystics have understood this truth, which is fundamental in much Eastern religion and philosophy. Ken Wilber points out that the Pure Ego or transcendental Ego of Western philosophers such as Kant (as opposed to the empirical ego) is identical with atma, pure awareness itself (*Sex, Ecology, Spirituality* 227–28). Furthermore, some Western philosophers such as Fichte hold that pure Ego is one with absolute spirit. This idea is identical with the Hindu formula Atman = Brahman; that is, the individual center of consciousness is one with the universal, all-encompassing divine consciousness.

Mystics East and West have realized their unity with the divine and have spoken of being instruments of divine will. Jakob Böhme, the seventeenth-century German mystic, composed an imaginary conversation between a student and a master who tells the student to stop willing and thinking so that he might come to know union with the divine (171):

1. The student said to the master: "How can I come to the supersensual life so that I can see God and hear him speak?" The master said: "If you can sweep up for a moment into that in which no creature dwells, you can hear what God speaks."

2. The student said: "Is that near or far?" The master said, "It is in you. If you could be silent from all willing and thinking for one hour you would hear God's inexpressible words."

3. The student said, "How can I remain silent in thinking and willing?" The master said: "When you remain silent from the thinking and willing of the self, the eternal hearing, seeing, and speaking will be revealed in you. . . . Your own hearing, willing, and seeing hinders you so that you do not see and hear God."

We must die to the personal will and even the transpersonal will for the highest will, the "will of God," to shine out. If we can open to the Source of being in deep silence, we realize that our little wills are encompassed by a universal, divine order. As Taimni asserts, we become "merely a center through which the Divine Will carries out, unhindered, the Divine Purpose" (190).

Böhme refers to stilling one's own separate will as "the resigned will." For him, resignation is not so much submissiveness or surrender as a calm letting go of one's personal agenda. In this state, the ordinary self is not so much diminished as it is greatly expanded with inner spaciousness. The personality and its concerns are no longer the focus; they recede in importance in a much vaster perspective. Böhme observes that resignation "does not kill you but makes you alive according to its life. Then you live, yet not you, but your will becomes its will" (180).

The resigned will does not imply inaction but rather inspired action. We bypass the personality and move from deep stillness directly into action, without the intermediate process of thinking and deciding in the personality. The lower will is swallowed in the universal will to the good for all beings. As Besant states, "The union of the separate Will with the one Will for the helping of the world is the goal which seems to be more worthy of reaching after than [any] the world can offer" (*Study in Consciousness* 282). It is indeed a worthy goal, for in conscious union with the One, the high purpose of human life is fulfilled.

Chapter 8

Ego and Atma:
The I and the All

[The divine spark] starts with divine consciousness; no past, no future, no separation. It is long before realizing that it is itself. Only after many births does it begin to discern by this collectivity of experience, that it is individual. At the end of its cycle of reincarnation it is still the same Divine Consciousness, but it has now become individualized Self Consciousness.

H. P. Blavatsky

When he was seventeen months old, Raun was diagnosed as profoundly autistic, severely dysfunctional, and retarded. His behavior was bizarre. He would spin around and around objects in a room. He would rock his body back and forth over and over. He would concentrate on a single object such as his hand for hours.

Raun had no communication with anyone. He never gestured meaningfully or pointed. He never made eye contact and was entirely mute, without a normal baby's vocalizations. He was oblivious to what was going on around him.

Raun never showed anger or anxiety but was gentle and soft. His parents called him their little Buddha who had been dropped from another planet. He was distant and encapsulated and lived in his own inner world, in "fantasies of his solitary universe," as his father described it.

Raun had a cognitive problem. The psychiatrist John Nelson's description of schizophrenia applies to him (40). Raun was generally unable to direct attention, to abstract what is important from what is not, or to place events in a meaningful context. He was unable to match new data with old or to generalize from one experience to the next; each new experience was disconnected from previous ones. He would discover his hand anew each day, apparently not recognizing it as part of his own body, or even that he had a body as an integrated whole. He was unable to form a coherent entity from the fragmented pieces of his isolated experiences. In autism, the ego fragments, as it does in schizophrenia, and the autistic have no sense of being one whole person. Raun had no ego—no sense of self as contrasted with another self or the world—as a reference point around which to organize and integrate experience. He showed no purposeful, organized behavior and no control over himself. Such a condition is very difficult to treat.

Raun's parents, both psychotherapists, decided to work with him full time. His two normal young sisters joined the team. They adjusted their lifestyle so that someone was with Raun at all times. They kept him in a small bathroom to protect him from sensory overload. They constantly tried to stimulate him to respond to them and the environment outside himself.

Raun gradually began to notice his family members. He made eye contact with them while being fed. He began to respond to the word *food* with excitement. A breakthrough came when he learned that crying could get him a drink or a door opened for him.

This was his first attempt to control his life. Another big step came when he learned to use words such as *wa* (for water) or *down* or *more* to get what he wanted. This triggered better control of his body and more purposeful behavior.

By the age of five, Raun no longer showed signs of autism. He became an intelligent, highly verbal, loving, curious little boy. Later he graduated cum laude from high school and then from an Ivy League university where he was passionately involved in politics, acting, debating, and tennis. Raun progressed from a helpless child with no sense of self to a successful extraverted individual with a strong sense of who he was (Kaufman 22–28).

Josh also had problems developing a healthy ego. Until he was ten, he and his parents lived at a Zen meditation center. At the age of seven, he impressed adults by meditating in the formal Zen position. He remembers his childhood as full of the smell of Japanese incense and images of serene Buddhas with half-closed lids, whose eternal bliss haunted him. He felt he had to be a god because only divinities got respect.

When meditators came for *sesshin,* periods of intense meditation, Josh had to eat alone because he was a distraction at the silent meals. During the adults' evening meditation, he stayed in a small room alone with no television. He drew pictures of Buddhas, along with Batman and Superman, and had a large picture of the Buddha in his room as well as a poster of a sports hero. He heard that Gautama had named his son Rahula, which means "fetter" or "bond." He wondered if the Buddha ever saw his son as more than a fetter. Josh's own mother spent long hours in meditation. When she asked the *roshi* or teacher if this was all right for her son, he said she was too attached to him and that it is good to be detached.

Josh read comic books based on the *jataka* tales about the Buddha's earlier incarnations as animals. Each adventure story had a moral: to think of others and never of yourself. Josh was taught from an early age that it was bad to want things for himself, that it was egotistical and a grave sin. He must want only to help others.

At fourteen, Josh took the Bodhisattva vow to devote himself wholly to helping all sentient beings find enlightenment. This ideal was so deeply ingrained in him that he felt happy and complete only when he was doing good (Shrei 10, 13).

Josh's orientation might suggest a person who has transcended self-centeredness and learned to be selfless. However, when he was much older, Josh realized that he was not genuinely selfless or giving but was "being good" from conditioning and guilt. He wrote that it was only after he had created a strong sense of self that he felt he could really utilize the Buddhist teachings to their fullest and be genuinely giving and self-forgetful. Before that insight, he had a sense of self, of being someone distinct from others, but conditioned to try to be selfless. Unlike Raun, he did have an ego, but it was not allowed to develop naturally.

The Healthy Ego

We all need to consolidate a well-defined sense of who we are. We need to distinguish between ourselves and others and to develop our own center, separate from others. We need to know what we feel and to be able to express it assertively. Otherwise, we will be dependent, clinging, and jealous. The psychotherapist and meditation teacher Jack Engler says, "One has to be somebody before one can be nobody. . . . The attempt to bypass the developmental task of identity formation . . . through a misguided spiritual attempt to 'annihilate the ego' has fateful and pathological consequences. . . . Both a sense of self and a sense of no-self—in that order—seem to be necessary to realize that state of optimal psychological well-being . . . the Buddha described as the end of suffering" (Vaughan, "In the Meantime" 132).

According to therapists like Engler, people with a strong ego have an inner core of strength to face the world. They are self-reliant, independent, and able to cope. Their self-esteem is high. They can have healthy relationships and set boundaries, not letting others take advantage of them, yet they are cooperative and empathetic. Those with weak egos, in contrast to the conventional stereotype, tend to be self-centered, narcissistic, and egocentric. They have low self-esteem and crave love. They are gullible, and easily victimized, helpless, and may be addictive. They blame others when things go wrong in their lives and are defensive. According to Jack Kornfield, a psychotherapist and meditation teacher, "When our sense of self-worth is low, we cannot set limits, make boundaries, or respect our own needs. Our seemingly compassionate assistance becomes mixed with dependence, fear and insecurity" (215).

Views of Ego

The word *ego* is difficult to pin down, as it has many meanings in different contexts. In ordinary use, according to *Merriam-Webster's Collegiate Dictionary*, *ego* means simply "the self," especially "as contrasted with another self or the world," but it also means "egotism" and "self-esteem." Freud used the word for that part of the mind that is conscious as opposed to the id and superego, which are unconscious. For him the id was the hostile and lustful aspects of ourselves that we are afraid to admit into awareness, like the anger you feel for your boss when he criticizes your work, or your lustful attraction to someone young and flirtatious. Freud discovered that the way to health for some of his patients was in becoming aware of this repressed material. He said, "Where there was id, there shall be ego."

C. G. Jung took the ego to be a limited part of a larger matrix, the self, that extends far beyond one's immediate awareness. Jung himself had a "personality number 2," a venerable figure whom he called Philemon, who had knowledge and wisdom that his conscious self had never known.

Ken Wilber defines the ego as a band of consciousness that comprises our role, our picture of ourselves, or our self-image, as well as the analytical and discriminatory nature of the intellect (the concrete mind, in Theosophical terminology). For him, the ego includes things like your pride at doing a good job, your disappointment at having a big nose, your shame at getting too angry with your child, as well as the way you divide up the world into separate, independent things.

The psychologist Erik Erikson has a positive view of ego. He says that it is the "consolidation that begins in young adulthood as a sense of being a person, able to manifest competently in work and in relationships, which then continues to develop throughout the rest of one's life" (Vaughan, "In the Meantime" 132). Ego in Erikson's sense is an important aspect of mental health, a function we all need to get along in the world.

In Theosophical writings, *Ego* is often capitalized to mean the individuality or transpersonal self. But it can also refer to the separative, egotistic self. Blavatsky says, "It is Kama-Manas or the lower Ego, which, deluded into a notion of independent existence . . . becomes Ego-ism, the selfish self" (*Collected Writings* 12:631).

In this book, the word *ego* is generally used to mean the sense of being a distinct, separate person that exists at the level of the personality and depends on the body, emotions, and lower mind. However, *ego* is not synonymous with the personality, which can exist in both pathological states and transcendent realizations without a sense of ego.

Development of Self-Sense

Today, psychologists tend to call the sense of being a distinct person "self-sense" rather than ego. Computers have no sense of self, no emotion, no values, no sense of being alive, no ego. As studies by Broughton have indicated (see chapter 2), we have not always had a self-sense. Piaget, who studied cognitive development in children, recognized that an ego center develops in stages. At first, babies do not recognize that they have a self apart from the environment. In self-recognition tests, a large spot of rouge is put on a baby's forehead, and a mirror is placed before the baby. Those of eighteen months and younger show no recognition of the reflection as themselves. Some look behind the mirror for another baby. When older toddlers see their reflection, they touch the red spot on their own forehead, showing that they recognize the image as themselves. In reviewing this and other studies, Morton Hunt writes: "The ability to consider one's self—what has been called self-awareness or referential self—is one of the last features of the self to emerge, occurring in the last half of the second year of life. . . . [It] is the cognitive capacity that allows for all self-conscious emotions such as embarrassment" (372).

Children develop an increasingly sophisticated sense of self. At early ages, they think everyone sees and feels as they see and feel, like the loving little boy who gave his mother the best present in the whole world, his pet frog. Young children don't differentiate themselves from others. Later they develop *metacognition,* which is an awareness of their own thought process and the ability to manage it. This is the beginning of a sense of being an independent self, apart from others and from the environment.

Order and Ego

Douglas Kraft, a Unitarian minister, Buddhist practitioner, and psychotherapist, sees human intelligence as the basis of self. He, like

Blavatsky, sees intelligence and order as a major characteristic of the human mind and meaning as a distinguishing human characteristic. As discussed in chapter 2, the mind gives meaning and significance to the stream of sensations, thoughts, and feelings that pour through it.

FIGURE 3

What do you see in figure 3? Triangles and circles? Look again. There are no triangles and no circles in the figure. Your mind has filled in blank spaces to create them. You saw things that are not there so that you could order the pieces into a meaningful pattern.

We have a need to give meaning to sensations and ideas. Do you find it hard to identify figure 4? Do you feel dissatisfied and confused when you look at it? You may have expected a tuning fork, but this strange shape sprouts three prongs instead of the anticipated two. You can't put it into any familiar category. You can't find meaning in it. Many people feel like this when they encounter dissonant music or nonobjective art.

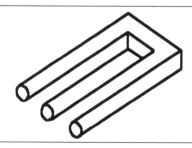

FIGURE 4

Kraft holds that in trying to find meaning we string together thoughts, feelings, and sensations, and we cluster them into a sense of self. In his Buddhistic view, the self does not exist independently—rathe,r we create it by tying memories together to create a sense of self from the flow of experience. We do this because of our urge to order things into meaningful wholes. Kraft says, "Objectively, we experience sights, sounds, thoughts, and feelings, and subjectively, we create a self sense to organize all these phenomena into a 'solid' entity. Self is, in part, the subjective experience of the mind's instinct to clump things together" (55).

The clumping Kraft talks of has been compared to the way we see the Big Dipper, which is a collection of unrelated stars at different distances from the Earth. Yet we organize these disparate points of light into a pattern. Our mental tendency to organize such separate elements into a meaningful whole does not negate organization in nature, such as the periodic table of elements in chemistry, the three-dimensional symmetry of crystals, or perhaps even unity among stars in a constellation considered from an astrological point of view. The mind does not produce such things but discovers and recognizes them.

The Fluctuating Ego

Despite the unreal nature of the ego, we usually feel we are an independent self, connected with a physical body. This self-sense is what the little boy Raun had not yet developed. If you feel angry and self-righteous, you feel that *you* are a self with principles that have been violated. If you are frightened, there is a strong sense of *yourself* being apart from the scary situation at hand. Most of us would feel as Liz Taylor did before a proposed operation for a brain tumor. She revealed her sense of identity in a *Life Magazine* interview when she said, "They wanted to operate on my brain—on my emotions, my thoughts, my memories, my sense of poetry, my feeling of colors, my soul, my self!" For her, "soul" and "self" were obviously aspects of her brain and personality, her lower self.

You feel *you* are the one who is angry or afraid. But in quieter, peaceful moments, or when you are wholly absorbed in a task or a line of thought or an uplifting emotion, you are less likely to experience a strong sense of ego. In meditation or while you are enjoying nature or are relaxed and in harmony with loved ones, the ego becomes lighter or even irrelevant. Ego comes and goes from moment to moment. The psychiatrist Stanislov Grof finds, "In essence, we do not have a fixed identity and can experience ourselves as anything on the continuum between the embodied self and Absolute Consciousness" (Schlitz 54).

The French philosopher René Descartes, who said, "I think, therefore I am," is the subject of a story in which he was invited to a dinner party one evening. When his hostess asked him if he wanted another cup of coffee, he said, "I think not," and disappeared! This joke holds some truth: we think ourselves into being a separate self. When the concept of a separate self goes, so does the experience of hard-edged ego.

The insight by Kraft and Gautama Buddha into the nature of self has been confirmed by many meditators through introspection. The meditation teacher Jean Klein (37) says, "'you' and 'I' as body and mind appear and disappear each with its own qualities, but they are nothing other than a collection of memories which have no existence in themselves. Just as waves and foam are nothing but sea, as separate entities they have only a temporary existence" (37). By observing one's stream of consciousness, one can perceive only a changing flux of sensations, feelings, thoughts, and images. Trying to catch a stable, continuing self in this flow reminds one of the photographer who tried to take a close-up of the horizon.

What we call our self is usually an identification of the "I" with some transient idea, feeling, or sensation such as "I am hungry," or

"I believe in being honest." Or we think of ourselves as a business person, a mother, an efficient worker, a failure, a golfer, a loving person. Our self-image and our roles in life, plus the continuity of our emotions and mental habits, make up a false sense of who we are. The sense of I "is only the pin which holds together memories and experiences in one composite whole," as Taimni asserts (122). There is no constant, definite self that sustains them. There is no little me inside that pops up and says, "Here I am!"

The British philosopher David Hume said: "When I enter most intimately into what I call *myself,* I always stumble on some particular perception or other, of heat or cold, light or shade, love or hatred, pain or pleasure. I never catch *myself* at any time without a perception, and never can observe anything but a perception" (Wilber, *Spectrum of Consciousness* 79). Hume concluded he was "nothing but a bundle or collection of different perceptions, which succeed each other with an inconceivable rapidity, and are in a perpetual flux and movement" (Goldstein and Kornfield 60). Jack Kornfield discovered the same thing: "There is no entity separate from the flow of experience, no 'self' to whom it is happening" (Goldstein and Kornfield 144).

Theosophy and the Buddhistic Ego

Meditators through the ages have confirmed that they experience no abiding entity within the stream of consciousness, no stable self at that level of experience. The lack of such a self is the *anatta* doctrine of Buddhism, which holds that everything is interdependent and nothing can exist as a separate being. The ego as an independent, separate self apart from the whole is an illusion, a fantasy built up unconsciously over lifetimes. It is not that we are simply caught in self-centeredness; there is no real separate self to be caught in. Someone asks, "Why are you unhappy? Because 99.9 percent of everything you think and feel and do is for self—and there isn't any." A cartoon captures this idea by showing a slipper-clad Sigmund Freud sitting in his chair with a cigar and a notepad in hand. Above the couch next to him, the Buddha is levitating. Freud asks, ". . . and how do you feel about not having a self?" Since Gautama has no self, we might ask, Who is the "you" Freud is addressing?

The Buddha's insight that our ordinary sense of being a separate self is based on illusion is radical; such insight can be life-changing. Yet there *is* within us something unique and individual that is more lasting. The specific character and destiny that we develop for ourselves over many lifetimes is not permanent. But behind the ongoing stream of experience is the Buddha nature, the inner faculty for enlightenment—atma and the transpersonal Self. Kornfield says that when the Buddha nature and the personal self "are combined with a deep realization of the emptiness of self [personality] we can be said to have fully discovered the nature of [transpersonal] self. This true [transpersonal] self is both unique and universal, both empty and full" (*Path with Heart* 212). Our egotistic self is transient and empty of any real, lasting core. But the transpersonal Self is more lasting. And our deepest being lies in what the Buddha called the changeless, the unborn, the unconditioned (Goddard 32–33)—what we have been calling "atma."

The Lankavatara Sutra explains that which is universal and yet unique (Goddard 305–307). It gives a view of human nature that can be mapped onto the Theosophical threefold view presented in this book. In this Buddhist model, the personality consists of the five elements (aggregates or skandhas: corporeality, feelings, perceptions of the discriminating mind, volition which creates mental formations, and consciousness of all the others). These impermanent functions make up the "mortal mind" or "individual discriminating mind," which corresponds to the outlook of the lower mind that sees differences and separateness.

The sutra also describes Universal Mind that transcends the personal, individualistic view point and is not involved in egoism: "Universal Mind ... transcends all individuation and limits. Universal mind is essentially pure in its essential nature, subsisting unchanged and free from faults of impermanence, undisturbed by egoism, unruffled by distinction, desires and aversions. . . . It is devoid of personality and all that belongs to it" (Goddard 306). Universal Mind as described here answers to our familiar term "atma," which is not the rigidly defined self that the Buddha denied but pure, boundless consciousness.

The Lankavarta goes on to describe the "intuitive mind" as between Universal Mind and mortal or discriminating mind. Its cause and support is Universal Mind, but it also relates to individual mind as it "shares its experiences and reflects upon its activities" (Goddard 307). Intuitive mind partakes in both transcendental intelligence with Universal Mind (atma) and differentiated knowledge with the individual discriminating (lower) mind. Thus it is both universal and unique. "The discriminating-mind is a dancer and a magician with the objective world as his stage. Intuitive-mind is the wise jester who travels with the magician and reflects upon his emptiness and transciency" (Goddard 307). This "intuitive mind" is the transpersonal self, a major component of which is buddhi or intuition.

Lama Govinda speaks of this overlapping of the individual empirical consciousness with the universal as due to the double character of manas (*Foundations* 75), which Theosophy designates higher and lower mind. The mind is the cause of error when directed to individual self-consciousness but the source of highest wisdom when facing Universal Mind. It can bind or liberate; that is, bind one to the limited view of a separated self or liberate one into the boundlessness of Universal mind, atma. Govinda describes two experiences that suggest these two viewpoints: "The difference in the effect of these two directions may be compared to the vision of a man, who observes the manifold forms and colours of a landscape and feels himself different from it (as 'I' and 'here')—and the vision of another one who gazes into the depths of the firmament, which frees him of all object-perception and thus from the awareness of his own self as well, because he is only conscious of the infinity of space or of 'emptiness'. His 'I' here loses its position through lack of contrast or opposition, finding neither anything to grasp nor from which to differentiate itself." Lower mind, because of its function of segregating and dividing, creates a sense of a separate self, while higher mind synchronized with buddhi releases one into awareness of the limitless expanse of consciousness or atma.

The Lankavatara refers to this change in perception as "turning about in the deepest seat of consciousness." Govinda describes it as a reorientation from the outer world of objects to the inner world of oneness, "a reversal of the direction of our inner vision from the manifold to the unified, from the limited to the unlimited, from the intellectual to the intuitive" (77). This new attitude means directing attention to the primordial source of our being, which is also the universal source of all consciousness. In this turning about, the illusion of the ego concept becomes apparent, though one continues to live in the world as a personality. Yet after this insight, Govinda says, even when contemplating the small and individual, one's connection with the whole is not lost, and one does not fall again into the error of egohood.

Moving Beyond Ego

Yet the ego or self-sense is a part of the whole that is necessary to focus the mind at certain stages of evolution. But we get caught in the ego, thinking it is all there is. Ego has been called a little that thinks it is the whole show. John Nelson says the ego is a tiny fragment of human nature, a subset of capabilities for the limited purpose of dealing with worldly matters. On the positive side, ego organizes our intelligence, gives us a sense of self, and gives coping powers for managing in the world. On the negative side, it can lead us into egotism, arrogance, and isolation from others.

Rewards to the ego are never enough. After seeking more and more material comforts, success, power, and prestige, many people still feel empty, experiencing a divine discontent or hunger for another dimension of experience. We glimpse that we are much more than the ego and yearn for something beyond its gratification. Frances Vaughan says that from the soul's point of view, the ego is a tiny island on a vast ocean of experience.

When touched by the transpersonal Self, the ego is quiet. We sometimes reach beyond our usual selves and have shining moments that transcend our usual way of being. Within us well up impersonal thoughts that are deep and broad, intuitive understanding, direction from the spiritual will, and intimations of divine presence.

Perhaps you have been struck by the truth of a spiritual teaching, such as the existence of deeper aspects to your mind or the realization that you have lived on earth before. Or you may have had moments of creativity when you easily found solutions that had evaded you before. You may have visited a nursing home or a hospital and been overwhelmed by compassion, far beyond what you usually feel. Or you may have been able to stick to a resolution to change, which you thought you would break, as though you called on a will beyond your personal willing. You may have felt moments of oneness with a transcendent presence.

At such moments of insight, it may seem as if we had been hanging for dear life onto the strap of a subway train, but discover we can let go and balance ourselves in a much freer way. We loosen our hold on ego and enter into what Jack Kornfield calls openness and nonseparation, which we experience when all the small and fixed notions of ourselves have been seen through and are dissolved. At such moments, we call out our transpersonal powers, our unique potentials. Robert Browning described this inner potential when he wrote in *Paracelsus,*

> There is an inner center in us all
> Where truth abides in fullness,
> . . . and to know
> Rather consists in opening out a way
> Whence the imprisoned splendour may escape
> Than in effecting entry for a light
> Supposed to be without.

C. G. Jung was in touch with such an inner center in himself. He wrote in his autobiography:

> Somewhere deep in the background I always knew that I was two persons. . . . Besides the world of the schoolboy, there existed another realm, like a temple in which everyone who entered became transformed and suddenly overpowered by a vision of the whole cosmos, so that he could only marvel and admire, forgetful of himself. Here lives the 'Other' who knew God as a hidden, personal, and at the same time suprapersonal secret. (47)

Our Higher Potentials

The idea of a higher self has invaded even the funny papers. An episode of "Doonesbury" shows a teenage girl at the beach with her boyfriend, who is wearing his football helmet while lying on the sand. She tells him that her past-life experiences might make more sense to him if he himself would access his "karmic core." All he has to do is to ask himself who he really is in his present incarnation. He says, "Easy. I'm a third string quarterback." She says that is fine, but what about his higher, spiritual self? "A first string quarterback." Delighted, she tells him, "See, you do recognize the god within!"

This "god within" at the level of the transpersonal Self is the source of our untapped spiritual potentials and special abilities. Jean Houston calls this hidden potential *entelechy,* a word from the Greek that implies purposeful unfoldment, as an acorn becoming an oak tree. "Beyond the surface of the literal seems to be the self's larger vision and comprehension of itself. This larger vision makes itself known as an entelechy, the dynamic purposefulness and full capacity of a person that is contained almost as an autonomous self within the self" (180).

According to Theosophy, we have unfolded our powers over many lifetimes and will continue to do so. Abilities gained from the past that we are not at present expressing, as well as unimagined future possibilities latent within atma and the transpersonal Self, are deep within us and can be called into action.

Our individual entelechy may be thought of as a field with far greater potential than we have yet discovered. We awaken these possibilities as we explore new and deeper ways of being. We will continue to grow into this archetype of who we are and what we can be as we, as pilgrims, travel through the rounds of evolution by means of reincarnation. As Christine Grof expressed her experience of her inner potential, she glimpsed

a larger force in my life which had become obscured, even with years of spiritual searching and different kinds of practices. This larger force is benevolent, always present. . . .

It's an aspect of who I am and of who everyone is. You could call it God, or Higher Power; there are many names for it. I began to consistently experience this enduring presence at work in myself, and I developed a trust in this spiritual force that I never had before. (49)

The relationship between the personality and the individuality or transpersonal Self is diagrammed in figure 5. The overlap between the personal self and transpersonal Self widens and deepens as the personality opens to higher influences.

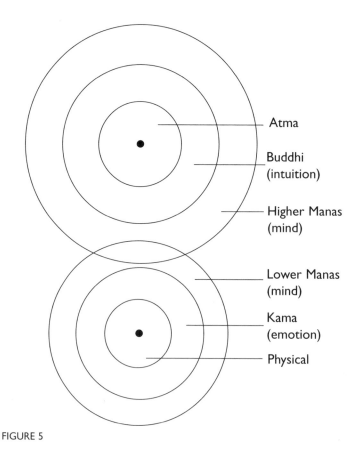

Atma

Buddhi
(intuition)

Higher Manas
(mind)

Lower Manas
(mind)

Kama
(emotion)

Physical

FIGURE 5

Ego and Evolution

Theosophy teaches that it has taken unimaginable eons of evolution for us to develop our personality and a well-defined sense of self, the sense of "I" that Taimni calls the essence and root of personality. We start our pilgrimage immersed in the One Life in which we have our being. Slowly, through eons of cyclic evolution, as the fields at various levels emerge from a homogeneous state, the planet and ourselves become more densified, defined, and focused. As the earth solidifies, we progress within the many fields it embodies. The mind becomes more focused, and we lose the sense of oneness we began with. We build up an ever-increasing sense of being an independent unit of consciousness as we release more and more of the immense powers of atma in the world.

Blavatsky says that we have recently passed the lowest point of this outward or downward development, called "involution," as spirit or consciousness becomes involved more and more deeply in matter. The human race as a whole has started the upward turn of the cycle, our aeonic journey back to oneness.

With little experience of ourselves as separate individuals, we evolve from a tribal consciousness that is not yet fully individualized but still immersed in the collective. At some point, a sense of individuality begins to dawn. As we develop the powers of the mind, we move into a sense of being an isolated ego. Then we transcend the mind; that is, we include it in the larger whole of our unified being. We experience individualness without *being* exclusively that individual. We return to oneness, but now with an awareness of ourselves as a center in the One Life. All of this development occurs within and against the backdrop of the vast, boundless consciousness that is our true being. Our models of what we are—or think we are—keep us from recognizing our limitless nature. As the Vedanta er Gangaji said on an audiotape, "Who you think you are is not who you are. The ego is essentially nonexistent. You are this vast, limitless, radiant consciousness" (Gangaji, New Dimensions Radio).

Individually, we are at different stages of the journey. Some of us are already beginning to move into a sense of unity, while others continue to develop through a strong sense of self. But eventually we will all again realize unity while still retaining the focus of mind and the powers that developed along the way.

The cycle of the human race from oneness through separated multiplicity to individualized oneness is repeated in miniature in our development from birth to old age. We have seen that the baby slowly develops a sense of self. Then for a time we operate with a strong sense of "me" and "mine." Only at mature stages do we learn how to be both an individual center and part of the larger whole of the community, nation, and world.

Ken Wilber points out that the stage of collective consciousness before we develop ego is often mistaken for our mature return to oneness, when ego is transcended, because genuine self-transcendence is confused with self-negation. This error is "the pre-trans fallacy" in which pre-conceptual oceanic feelings are confused with post-conceptual insight into the unitary background of "individualized Self-consciousness," in Blavatsky's words.

As explained, evolution develops all our powers, including those of the personality. On our return to oneness, we do not destroy the abilities of our body, mind, and emotion. Rather, we expand their use from only personal abilities and put them instead in the service of purposes larger than our egoistic satisfaction. The Theosophical author Gottfried de Purucker advises, "Do not annihilate your personality in the sense of wiping it out. You have brought into being yourself; it is a part of you, . . . the evolutionary work of aeons in the past. Raise the personality. Cleanse it, train it, make it shapely and symmetrical . . . discipline it . . . so that it shall become . . . a clean and pure channel for passing into the human consciousness the rays of glory streaming from the god within" (14).

Transcending the Ego

As we move from strong individualism into a growing sense of the whole, we still need ego strength based on knowing our boundaries. The ego as self-sense will always be part of who we are as human beings; we will not completely eliminate it. But as Frances Vaughan points out, to transcend means to include in a larger whole: "Transcending ego does not mean obliterating ego and becoming dysfunctional. It means expanding the sense of identity to include more than is designated as ego. Ego identity must be claimed before it can be released" (*Shadows* 238).

A mature person has a healthy self-sense without being egocentric. We will learn to use the mind and emotions, indeed all the powers of the personality, with less egotism. *Merriam-Webster's Collegiate Dictionary* give three senses for *egotism*: (1) "excessive use of the first person singular personal pronoun"; (2) "the practice of talking about oneself too much" (and we might add thinking about oneself too much, as in the Alcoholics Anonymous slogan, "I may not be much, but I'm all I ever think about"); (3) "an exaggerated sense of self-importance: conceit," like the person who said, "I'm not conceited, though I have every right to be."

Another aspect of egotistic conceit is seeing only from one's own point of view. Ego as self-sense necessarily includes the unique stance from which we meet the world. But when we feel strongly that "I am right and you are wrong," we are caught in egotism, an ego-centered view. It is rare that one point of view is completely right and another completely wrong. In the pluralistic society in which we live, we especially need to be open to views other than our own and to avoid being entrenched in a single narrow perspective. As the world becomes a "global village," we increasingly need to empathize with and understand our fellow villagers.

The sixteenth-century Copernican revolution showed that the sun, not the earth, is the center of our solar system. We need a twenty-first-century Copernican revolution to show that the transpersonal Self, not the ego or personality, is the center of our being.

Swami Beyondananda is a fictitious guru full of wisdom and humor. A devoted disciple implored him, "O Guru, tell us the shortest path to enlightenment." The wise one sat in silence with eyes closed for a while. Then he gazed at his disciple and said simply, "Ego, ego-ing, e-gone." Until we reach the "e-gone" stage, we may find ego both coming and going, hopefully with more going than coming.

Realizing the Whole of Ourselves

Catherine Ingram, a teacher of meditation, says that trying to overcome attachment to the ego in our usual state of mind is like trying to draw water from a mirage. The seemingly separate self is an illusion that has no lasting reality. But Ingram warns against pretending some kind of lofty detachment or "up-leveling" to avoid pain. This leads only to denial or repression. How, then, can we see beyond the walls we have constructed around ourselves and glimpse the greatness beyond? Ingram advises, "Have intention not to indulge your 'I' story. Pop out of your trance as soon as you notice being lost in it. Drop the illusory myth of I, me, mine" (78).

Acting on such an intention begins with self-awareness. This is not the same as self-preoccupation when you are overly concerned with your business affairs, your health, what others think of you, or any of your personal concerns. Rather, it means knowing what your motivations are and what you are feeling, thinking, and sensing. When you are in this mode, you are aware if you slip into self-pity, or conceit in thinking your view is the only right one, or escape from responsibility by blaming your problems on a difficult childhood. The practice of mindfulness can gradually reveal the workings of the "I" process by which we create our identity as a separate self. It is not easy to break this long-held habit. Yet as the Buddhist teacher Lama Govinda says, "Consciousness is a living stream which cannot be caught in the vessel of a narrow ego. . . . When individuality thus loses its conscious relationship with universality and tries to become an end in itself by clinging to its momentary existence, the illusion of a changeless separate ego is created, the flow is arrested, and stagnation sets in" (*Way of the White Clouds* 124).

But even gaining insight into the causes of ego does not automatically dissolve the unconscious identification of yourself with your ego. It takes a long time for a deeply ingrained habit to die. A good beginning in opening to something beyond your usual confines is from time to time to observe your stream of consciousness without interfering. This helps you detach from your usual identifications. Then in moments of inner stillness, try to experience your consciousness devoid of content. As advised in the Buddhist verses of "Tilopa's Song to Naropa," "Cut through the roots of complexity with the sharp gaze of naked awareness, remaining entirely at peace, transparent and content" (Hixon 252). In tasting atma, pure consciousness, boundaries dissolve and you are lost in the boundless all. In this realization, you might discover that what you are is not the ego, but the consciousness that contains everything.

Yet, as we have seen, Mahayana Buddhism and Theosophy teach a stable center at a level deeper than ego or the self-sense of the personality: that "sacred spark which burns and expands into the flower of human reason and self-consciousness" (*Secret Doctrine*

2:95). This "spark" is the combination of atma and buddhi that Blavatsky calls the monad (as mentioned in chapter 1). You might think of the monad as your own particular point or localization in a shoreless ocean of light, the unfading light of atma whose shadows create your individual being.

The Katha Upanishad says that atma is smaller than the small and greater than the great. It has the paradoxical characteristic of being an unbroken continuum yet a dimensionless point. As N. Sri Ram, author and former president of the Theosophical Society, says, "Our consciousness as subject or 'knower' as a center of action is a dimensionless point and at the same time an expanse" (182). As atma, we are a universal, boundless field, one with the essence of all that is. As ego, we encapsulate the point aspect of atma within the here and now of our personal concerns, time-bound. We are both the continuum of atma and the time-bound ego. These are two opposite poles of our being.

The atmic center or monad emanates the individuality or transpersonal Self, which in turn emanates the personality. The transpersonal Self is a semi-permanent center that serves as a transformer of the high voltage of atma. It steps down atma so that it can power the personality, for the monad is "the irradiating spirit of every human being" (*Secret Doctrine* 1:120). We usually experience ourselves as the stepped-down personality, not as the individual transpersonal Self or the monad. As we work through the personality, which we are destined to do, we may get lost in ego and separateness. Yet ultimately we are always atma and the monad, the spiritual ground of our being. Our true identity is in the monad, the "bright star dropped from the heart of eternity," as Blavatsky stated (*Secret Doctrine* 1:120).

The Theosophical teacher Geoffrey Hodson taught a meditation he called "A Yoga of Light" to help us recall who we are. Try the following slightly modified form of that meditation after some deep breaths and quieting your mind. Repeat each affirmation to yourself, leaving spaces of silence between them. When you finish the affirmations, just rest in the silence for a while.

> I am not only the body that lives and dies,
> I am the Self within.
> I am not only the emotions that constantly change,
> I am the Self within.
> I am not only the thoughts that come and go,
> I am the Self within.
> I am the silent Self, the abiding Self, the Self of deep peace,
>   at one with all.
> I am that Self.
> That Self am I.

References

Achterberg, Jeanne. *Use of Symbol and Ritual in Healing.* Ojai, Calif.: Krotona School of Theosophy (audio tape), 1997.

Anderson, William. "The Great Memory," *Noetic Science Review*, Spring 1992.

Armstrong, Ellen. "Bottom Line Intuition," *New Age*, December 1985.

Assagioli, Roberto. *The Act of Will.* Baltimore: Penguin, 1974.

Assagioli, Roberto. *Psychosynthesis.* New York: Hobbs, Dorman, 1965.

Besant, Annie. *The Self and Its Sheaths.* Adyar, Madras, India: Theosophical Publishing House, 1948.

———. *A Study in Consciousness.* Adyar, Madras, India: Theosophical Publishing House, 1938.

———. *Thought Power.* Wheaton, Ill: Theosophical Publishing House, 1988.

Besant, Annie, and C. W. Leadbeater. *Thought Forms.* Wheaton, Ill.: Theosophical Publishing House, 1994.

Blavatsky, Helena Petrovna. *The Collected Writings.* 15 vols. Wheaton, Ill.: Theosophical Publishing House, 1977–91.

———. *The Key to Theosophy.* London: Theosophical Publishing House, 1889.

———. *The Secret Doctrine.* 3 vols. Wheaton, Ill.: Theosophical Publishing House, 1993.

———. *The Theosophical Glossary.* Los Angeles: Theosophy Co., 1930.

———. *The Voice of the Silence.* Wheaton, Ill.: Theosophical Publishing House, 1992.

Böhme, Jakob. *The Way to Christ.* New York: Paulist Press, 1978.

Burnier, Radha. *The Way of Self-Knowledge.* Adyar, Madras, India: Theosophical Publishing House, 1979.

Chari, V. K. *Whitman in the Light of Vedantic Mysticism.* Lincoln, Nebr.: University of Nebraska Press, 1970.

Chatterji, J. C. *The Wisdom of the Vedas*. Wheaton, Ill.: Theosophical Publishing House, 1973.

Codd, Clara. *The Way of the Disciple*. Adyar, Madras, India: Theosophical Publishing House, 1974.

Collins, Mabel. *Light on the Path*. Wheaton, Ill.: Theosophical Publishing House, 1980.

Csikszentmihalyi, Mihaly. *Flow: The Psychology of Optimal Experience*. New York: Harper, Perennial, 1990.

Deikman, Arthur. "The Spiritual Heart of Service," *Noetic Science Review*, Winter 1997.

Dossey, Larry. *Healing Words*. San Francisco: Harper, 1993.

———. *Meaning and Medicine*. New York: Bantam Books, 1991.

———. *Space, Time and Medicine*. Boulder, Colo.: Shambhala, 1982.

Emery, Marcia. *Intuition Workbook*. Englewood Cliffs, N.J.: Prentice Hall, 1994.

Easwaran, Eknath, trans. *The Upanishads*. Tomales, Calif.: Nilgiri Press, 1987.

Gangaji. "Who Are You?" New Dimensions Radio Tape, #2609, 1996.

Goddard, Dwight. *A Buddhist Bible*. Boston: Beacon Press, 1970.

Goldberg, Philip. *The Intuitive Edge*. New York: Tarcher, Putnam's, 1983.

Goldstein, Joseph, and Jack Kornfield. *Seeking the Heart of Wisdom*. Boston: Shambhala, 1987.

Goleman, Daniel. *Emotional Intelligence*. New York: Bantam, 1995.

Goswami, Amit. *The Self-Aware Universe*. New York: Tarcher, 1993.

———. *The Visionary Window*. Wheaton, Ill.: Theosophical Publishing House, 2000.

Govinda, Lama Anagarika. *Foundations of Tibetan Mysticism*. New York: Dutton, 1960.

———. *The Way of the White Clouds*. Berkeley: Shambhala, 1971.

Green, Elmer E. "Copper Wall Research: Psychology and Psychophysics." Proceeding for International Society for the Study of Subtle Energies and Energy Medicine, 1st Annual Conference, June 21–25, 1991, in Boulder, Colo.

Grof, Christina. "Spirituality and the Eternal Self: An Interview with Christina Grof," by Katherine Ziegler. *Quest*, Spring 1996.

Hankin, N. S. "The Creative Mind" in *The Theosophist*, Adyar, Vol. 119.4, Jan. 1998.

Hixon, Lex. *Mother of the Buddhas*. Wheaton, Ill.: Theosophical Publishing House, 1993.

Holst, Spencer. "Brilliant Silence." *Noetic Science Review*, 42, Summer 1997.

Houston, Jean. *A Mythic Life*. San Francisco: Harper, 1996.

Hunt, Morton. *The Story of Psychology*. New York: Doubleday, 1993.

Ingram, Catherine. 1995. "Thunderstorm in an Open Sky." *Quest* Magazine, Autumn 1995.

Jung, Carl G. *Memories, Dreams, Reflections*. New York: Pantheon, 1973.

Karagulla, Shafica, and Dora Kunz. *The Chakras and the Human Energy Fields*. Wheaton, Ill.: Theosophical Publishing House, 1989.

Kaufman, Neil. "SonRise: The Miracle Continues." *Noetic Science Review* #34, Summer 1995.

Keller, Evelyn Fox. *A Feeling for the Organism*. New York: W. H. Freeman and Co., 1983.

Khenpo, Nyoshul. *Natural Great Perfection*. Ithaca, N.Y.: Snow Lion, 1995.

King, Serge. *Earth Energies*. Wheaton, Ill.: Theosophical Publishing House, 1992.

Klein, Jean. *I Am*. Guernsey, Channel Islands: Third Millennium Publications, 1989.

Knaster, Mirka. *A Gentle Rain. Common Boundary* 15.5, Sept./Oct. 1997.

Kornfield, Jack. *A Path with Heart*. New York: Bantam, 1993.

————. "Take One Seat" Audiotape. Spirit Rock, Calif.: Insight Meditation West, 1990.

Kraft, Douglas C. B. "Shadows in the Mirror." *Quest* Magazine, Spring 1996.

Krieger, Dolores. *Accepting Your Power to Heal.* Santa Fe, N.M.: Bear, 1993.

Krieger, Dolores. *The Therapeutic Touch.* Englewood Cliffs, N.J.: Prentice Hall, 1979.

Krishnamurti, Jiddu. *At the Feet of the Master and Towards Discipleship.* Wheaton, Ill.: Theosophical Publishing House, Quest Books, 2001.

Kunz, Dora. *The Personal Aura.* Wheaton, Ill.: Theosophical Publishing House, 1991.

Leadbeater, Charles Webster. *The Chakras.* Wheaton, Ill.: Theosophical Publishing House, 1980.

The Mahatma Letters to A. P. Sinnett. Chronological ed. Quezan City, Philippines: Theosophical Publishing House, 1993.

Mascaro, Juan, trans. *The Upanishads.* Baltimore: Penguin Books, 1965.

Maslow, Abraham, H. *The Farther Reaches of Human Nature.* New York; The Viking Press, 1972.

————. *Motivation and Personality.* 3rd ed. Rev. Robert Frager. New York: Harper and Row, 1987.

May, Rollo. *Love and Will.* New York: Dell, 1969.

May, Rollo, Ernest Angel, and Henri F. Ellenberger, eds. *Existence: A New Dimension in Psychiatry and Psychology.* Northvale, N.J.: Aronson, 1994.

Merriam-Webster's New Collegiate Dictionary. 10th ed. Springfield, Mass.: Merriam-Webster, 1993.

Mishlove, Jeffrey. *New Physics and Beyond* (video). Oakland, Calif.: Thinking Allowed Productions, 1988.

Motoyama, Hiroshi. *Theories of the Chakras.* Wheaton, Ill.: Theosophical Publishing House, 1984.

Moyers, Bill. *The Language of Life.* New York: Doubleday, 1995.

Murphy, Michael. *The Future of the Body.* Los Angeles: Tarcher, 1992.

Nelson, John E. *Healing the Split.* Albany, N.Y.: State University of New York Press, 1994.

Nicholson, Shirley. *Ancient Wisdom—Modern Insight.* Wheaton, Ill.: Theosophical Publishing House, 1985.

Nikhilananda, Swami, trans. *Self-Knowledge.* New York: Ramakrishna-Vivekananda Center, 1974.

Pearl, Joseph H. "Piaget, Bergson, and the Mystical Experience." *The American Theosophist.* Vol. 7 no. 2, Feb. 1982, pp 30–35.

Prabhavananda, Swami, and Frederick Manchester, trans. *The Upanishads, Breath of the Eternal.* New York: The New American Library (a Mentor Book), 1957.

Purucker, Gottfried de. 1935. *Golden Precepts of Esotericism.* 3d and rev. ed. Pasadena, Calif.: Theosophical University Press, 1979.

Remen, Rachel Naomi. *Kitchen Table Wisdom: Stories That Heal.* New York: Riverhead, 1997.

Shallcross, J., and Dorothy A. Sisk. *Intuition: An Inner Way of Knowing.* Buffalo, N.Y.: Bearly Limited, 1989.

Schlitz, Marilyn, et al. "Toward a Noetic Model of Medicine." *Noetic Science Review,* Winter 1998, No. 47.

Sheldrake, Rupert. *A New Science of Life.* Los Angeles: J.P. Tarcher, 1981.

———. "Experiments on the Sense of Being." Stored at *Journal for the Society of Psychical Research.* April 2001.

Shrei, Josh. 1995. "Growing Up Zen in America." *Inquiring Mind* 12.1, Fall 1995.

Simonton, O. C., Stephanie Simonton, and J. Creighton. *Getting Well Again.* Toronto: Bantam Books, 1980.

Smith, Huston. *Forgotten Truth: The Common Vision of the World's Religions.* New York: Harper & Row, 1976.

Sri Ram, N. *Seeking Wisdom.* Adyar, India: Theosophical Publishing House, 1969.

Stevenson, Ian, M.D. *Where Reincarnation and Biology Intersect.* Westport, Conn.: Praeger, 1997.

Taimni, I. K. *A Way of Self-Discovery.* Wheaton, Ill.: Theosophical Publishing House, 1970.

Teilhard de Chardin, Pierre. *The Phenomenon of Man.* London: Collins, 1959.

Tiller, William. "New Fields, New Laws." In *Future Science,* ed. John White and S. Krippner. Garden City, N.J.: Doubleday, 1977.

Tower, Virginia. *The Process of Intuition.* Wheaton, Ill.: Theosophical Publishing House, 1987.

Vaughan, Frances. *Awakening Intuition.* New York: Doubleday, Anchor, 1979.

———. "In the Meantime . . ." *What Is Enlightenment,* Fall-Winter 1998.

———. *The Inward Arc.* Nevada City, Calif.: Blue Dolphin, 1985.

———. *Shadows of the Sacred.* Wheaton, Ill.: Theosophical Publishing House, 1995.

Wald, George. "Life and Mind in the Universe." *Theosophical Research Journal* 3.2, June 1986, 35–49.

Walsh, Roger, and Frances Vaughan, eds. *Paths Beyond Ego.* Los Angeles: J.P. Tarcher/Periges, 1993.

Wilber, Ken. *Sex, Ecology, Spirituality.* Boston: Shambhala, 1995.

———. *The Spectrum of Consciousness.* Wheaton, Ill.: Theosophical Publishing House, 1977.

———. "To See a World: Art and the I of the Beholder." *Journal of Transpersonal Psychology* 29.2, 1997.

Index

QUEST BOOKS

are published by
The Theosophical Society in America
Wheaton, Illinois 60189-0270,
a worldwide, nonprofit membership organization
that promotes fellowship among all peoples of the world,
encourages the study of religion, philosophy, and science,
and supports spiritual growth and healing.

Today humanity is on the verge of becoming, for the first time in its history, a global community. The only question is what kind of community it will be. Quest Books strives to fulfill the purpose of the Theosophical Society to act as a leavening; to introduce into humanity a large mindedness, a freedom from bias, an understanding of the values of the East and West; and to point the way to human development as a means of service, both for the individual and for the whole of humankind.

For more information about Quest Books,
Visit **www.questbooks.net**
For more information about the Theosophical Society,
visit **www.theosophical.org.**
or contact **Olcott@theosmail.net**
or (630) 668-1571.

*The Theosophical Publishing House is aided by
the generous support of the KERN FOUNDATION,
a trust dedicated to Theosophical education.*